UPTON
Portrait of a
Severnside Town

And now I mark where Upton's spires arise,
Whilst many stately trees, and many cots,
And villages, o'erspread the country round,
And orchards, with their odoriferous breath,
That scent the air, and to the eye present
One sheet of blossoms.

J. Cottle
A Poem on Malvern Hills, 1798

UPTON
Portrait of a Severnside Town

by
Pamela Hurle

with photographs by
John Talbot Cooper

PHILLIMORE

First published in 1979

Second edition, 1988
Published by
PHILLIMORE & CO. LTD.
Shopwyke Hall, Chichester,
Sussex, England

ISBN 0 85033 687 2

Printed and bound in Great Britain by
BILLING & SONS LIMITED

CONTENTS

LIST OF FIGURES

LIST OF PLATES

(between pages 32 and 33)

INTRODUCTION

Upton-upon-Severn has been a thriving little Worcestershire town for so long that it comes as something of a shock to realise how little of its history has been studied and made readily available to its inhabitants and visitors, many of whom arrive by the age-old route—the River Severn. It is hoped that this book, while satisfying the need for a brief and readable history based on reliable evidence, will stimulate enough interest to fill some of the gaps which inevitably still remain. No history is ever complete, for new material is constantly coming to light; but if this book fires even a few with enough enthusiasm to pursue further researches, or if it gives pleasure to those who would like to know something of Upton's past, it will have served its purpose.

The year 1979 marks the centenary of the opening of the Victorian church at the southern end of the town. The rector in 1879 was the Rev. Robert Lawson, whose wife was a devoted and knowledgeable chronicler of the town's history. Her books, *Records and Traditions of Upton-upon-Severn* (1869) and *The Nation in the Parish* (1884) make delightful and informative reading, but are rare now and obviously somewhat outdated. So it seems an appropriate time to produce a new history of the town in a modern format with photographs to illustrate some of the places round which Mrs. Lawson and her contemporaries moved, but which are, in some cases, now lost to us for ever. It is a particular pleasure to me to be able to include photographs from the collection of John Talbot Cooper: some are his own original pictures and others he has reproduced, with considerable skill and care, from old and sometimes rather battered pictures, which portray old Upton in a way that no words could possibly do. Unfortunately, despite his efforts, it has not always been possible to discover the original photographers of these scenes from the past: whoever they may have been, thanks are due to them—and also our apologies for being unable to name them. Many kind people loaned pictures for reproduction, and we thank Miss V. Cole, Mr. A. Cope, Mrs. J. F. Copson, Miss E. Denley, Mr. B. Edmondson, Mrs. G. Evans, Mrs. M. Fall, Mrs. Gainey, Miss E. Griffin, Mrs. C. Gurney, Mrs. Hazelwood, Mrs. A. Hill, Mr. E. Hunt, Mrs. K. Jones, Mr. W. Jones, Rev. D. Lockwood, Mrs. Muller, Mrs. A. Oakley, Mr. H. Panting, Mrs. M. Powell, Mr. B. Pratley, Mrs. J. and Miss C. Pratley, Mrs. C. Price, Mrs. A. E. Rose, Mrs. M. Stanton, Mrs. M. Talbot Cooper, Mr. F. G. Taylor, Mr. T. Taylor, Miss V. White, Miss P. Woodward, and Malvern Library.

Mr. A. T. Atkinson has drawn the two most useful maps of Upton in the 19th century, using as his guide the 1841 Tithe Map. I am most grateful to him for his skills, both in cartography and in deciphering what I was asking him to do. I would also like to thank Mr. E Hargrave for his drawing of Severn trows.

In writing this, my third local history, I have once again met many very kind and helpful people who have strengthened my conviction that there is an enormous interest in local history and a desire to share whatever information is available. My finished text inevitably bears the imprint of many, often brief, discussions with local men and women, as well of the hours studying the works listed in the bibliography. Some deserve special mention because their contributions, in the form of documents loaned or facts and opinions given, have helped to shape this book. The rector of Upton, the Rev. Anthony King, gave me free access to all the diverse and invaluable documents of which he is the custodian and some useful leads as to where I might find more: he has consistently offered me every facility for research, and I thank him very warmly. Father Watkins at St. Joseph's Catholic church and Mr. and Mrs. Wylie at the Baptist church have helped with the chapter on religious dissent in Upton, and Mr. D. B. Smith, headmaster of the primary school, also very kindly allowed me to use school records. I found Mr. Basil Edmondson, son of a former rector, a valuable walking encyclopaedia when I wanted to check numerous points. Mrs. Pumfrey and Mrs. Price, the wife and daughter of the late Mr. James Pumfrey, very kindly permitted me to see the copious notes which he had made on Upton in earlier times and, the Pumfreys being one of Upton's long-established families, this was both fascinating and helpful. I also wish to thank Miss F. Bramford, Miss R. Disley, Mrs. R. W. Guilding, Miss M. J. Hebden, Mr. C. J. Prosser, Mr. J. Thould, and Mrs. Wingfield.

The staff at the County Record Office and at Malvern and Worcester Libraries have, as always, given me all possible help: they usually manage somehow to meet what at first sight looks an impossible request. Miss Andrews, clerk to the Parish Council, and Mr. John Brailsford, with his skills at photocopying, have also been at hand to help in times of difficulty.

I must, of course, acknowledge my debt to Mrs. Lawson. The more I studied her books, parish records and other historical evidence, the greater became my respect for this remarkable woman who, despite failing eyesight, persevered with her self-imposed task of recording the history of the town she had grown to love. Writing at a time when local history was too often a boring and pretentious account of the pedigree of some local dignitary, she was too full of concern for the ordinary people around her to fall into that trap, so her books, even a hundred years later, can still teach any local historian a lot.

Finally, I thank my family: my husband, who has never failed to help and encourage me; and Kate and Clare, who have for years cheerfully tolerated their mother's passion for local history.

Pamela Hurle

January 1979

INTRODUCTION TO (1988) SECOND EDITION

This history of Upton went out of print some years ago, and I am grateful for the opportunity to bring it up-to-date with a second edition. It has not been possible – nor is it particularly desirable – to rewrite the whole book but this reprint makes it possible to comment on changes during the last ten years. No community stands still and although Upton has inevitably, like everywhere else, experienced some losses, it has also once more shown itself to bear that vital hallmark of the survivor – the ability to recognise and respond to changing attitudes and needs.

August 1988   Pamela Hurle

Chapter I

THE ORIGINS AND EARLY DEVELOPMENT OF UPTON

UPTON, ON THE BANKS of the Severn, lies 10 miles down-stream from Worcester, and 18 miles upstream from Gloucester. The fertile Vale of Evesham lies to the east, while five miles to the west the ridge of the Malvern Hills dominates the horizon. Thus Upton lies in the delightful south-western corner of a Midland county which boasts a long and important history in the agricultural, industrial and political life of the country.

The origins of Upton are as obscure as those of any other settlement, but its position on the River Severn was clearly crucial both in its establishment and its continued growth. The name itself is quite a common one, and in the case of Upton-upon-Severn probably derives from the fact that it was a settlement further up the Severn from Ripple, of which it once formed part and which probably has an older foundation. The Worcester historian, A. E. E. Jones, quoted from a charter of 680 concerning the grant of land in Ripple to the monk Frithwold, but the earliest written reference to Upton which has so far come to light is an inquiry made in 897. According to the researchers for the *Victoria County History* this inquiry seems to indicate that Upton was granted by the Mercian King Coenwulf to Winchcombe Abbey in the late eighth or early ninth century. The land subsequently fell to the bishopric of Worcester. In 962 the Bishop of Worcester—the energetic and saintly Oswald—granted six hides of land to the thegn Cynelm. This considerable acreage of land seems to have stretched from the river near Ham Court up to the parish boundary with Welland—indeed it followed much the same boundary as the present parish of Upton. By the 11th century the land had once more reverted to the bishopric. More than written evidence is required to build up a picture

1

of the development of any community. A 19th-century geologist identified a block of basalt at the corner of School Lane as having originated in North Wales. It was apparently conveyed to Upton as the icebergs gradually melted during the Ice Age. Probably there was later—but still in prehistoric times—a river crossing at Upton which would have made the settlement relatively important, and in Roman times it is possible that some defences were constructed on the hill near Southend Farm. The antiquary William Stukeley wrote in the mid-18th century:

> There was a road along the Severn from Worcester to Upton, where antiquities are dug up. I take the town to be the Upocessa of the Ravennas.

Speculation that the area was influenced by the Romans was encouraged by the curious discovery reported in 19th-century books: in 1787 a shepherd boy found a circular cavity in a cornfield and

> upon examination it was found to be the entrance to a cavern of considerable dimensions, sunk about ten feet below the surface, and extending in every direction about twenty feet. At about thirty or forty feet is a body of water, of the estimated depth of about one hundred and forty feet. Various conjectures originated from this discovery, some attributing these excavations to a convulsion of nature, others to the hand of art.

The more learned referred to the Roman historian Tacitus who wrote of the German practice of digging such caverns as refuges or as storerooms for crops during the frosty winter months. Others believed that the Romans buried their dead here, while the less romantic thought quite simply that such a cavern was a well or even a rubbish dump. The present author has so far been unable to identify the site of the cavern.

The Romans left Britain at the beginning of the fifth century and the history of Britain for the next few centuries is somewhat obscure. A succession of invaders less civilised than the Romans plundered or tried to settle in the fertile regions of the island, but in the midst of all the uncertainties of the time there is little that we can know about Upton. From the Malvern Hills across to the River Severn was part of the extensive forest land in which small communities settled from the earliest times, and we may well wonder what fate these communities suffered when, in the ninth century, the Danes, attracted by the fertile lands along the

Severn, invaded the area and left behind them a trail of damage and destruction. They advanced to Deerhurst, less than ten miles from Upton, and wrought such havoc that the inhabitants are reputed to have fled to the wilderness that was to become Malvern Chase. And legend has it that the citizens of Worcester were so incensed by the Danish attacks that they seized a Dane who had become separated from his companions and, having skinned him, nailed his skin to the cathedral door. We do not know how the Danish invasions affected Upton, but since the route to Worcester was up the Severn it would be remarkable if Upton were spared the attentions of these men, who took whatever they fancied from any community they passed. Only about four miles away from the river, in the parish of Welland, there is an area known as Danemore, and a map of 1633 shows a spot at Danemore marked 'Battell oke', so possibly the Danes ran through the settlement at Upton and met resistance at Welland.

By the time that Bishop Oswald made his grant to Cynelm in 962 the area in and around Upton—much of it in episcopal hands—was largely uncultivated forest land with clearings that had been fenced off and ploughed with rudimentary tools by the small groups of men and women who also made enclosures to protect their animals from the wolves which still prowled the woodland.

The first major piece of documentary evidence relating to Upton is in the Domesday Book drawn up in 1086 on the order of William the Conqueror. Upton is mentioned by name in this great survey, thus distinguishing it from its less noteworthy neighbours such as Welland. The Domesday entry for Ripple and Upton reads:

Facsimile, from Nash's *Worcestershire*, of the Domesday entry for Upton with Ripple.

The same Bishop (of Worcester) holds Ripple with Upton. There
are 25 hides that pay geld. Thirteen of these are in demesne, where
there are 4 ploughs; and there are 2 priests who have 1½ hides with
2 ploughs; there are 40 villeins and 16 bordars with 36 ploughs.
There are 8 serfs and one bondwoman and a mill and 30 acres of
meadow. The woodland is half a league long and three furlongs
wide and is in Malferna; the Bishop had the honey from it and the
hunting and all profits plus ten shillings; now it is part of the king's
forest; but the Bishop has the pannage and wood for firing and
repairs. It was and is worth £10.

Since this entry is a joint one for the whole of the manor it is
impossible to distinguish between Ripple and Upton, but,
nevertheless, it tells us quite a lot. Historians still argue about
the meaning of the term 'hide' and perhaps the most helpful
thing to say is that it was a unit of land measurement which
may have been about 120 acres, but its real importance was
as a means of assessing tax. A community paying tax on as
much as 25 hides would have been quite large and flourishing.
There were two priests so it seems likely that one would have
lived in and served Ripple, while the other was at Upton. No
church is mentioned, but doubtless there was at least one. The
priests held about six per cent. of the land, while the 13 hides
in demesne—over half the land—refer to the land retained by
the lord of the manor, in this case the Bishop of Worcester,
for himself. So the rest of the population lived off the remaining 10-and-a-half hides. The survey mentions only 67 people,
but the total population, including their families and dependants
would have been more than this. It is usual to multiply by four
or five the number of persons mentioned in order to arrive
at the total figure. This puts the total population of Ripple
and Upton together in the region of three hundred. The serfs
and bondwoman were little more than slaves, while the villeins
and bordars were somewhat higher in the social scale. They
were required to work on the demesne as a form of rent for
the land that they cultivated for their own livelihood, but they
enjoyed no security of tenure on their land and could be evicted
if the lord wished it. Apart from the two priests the manor
seems to have been inhabited by a purely peasant population,
with none of the higher ranks of society holding land, except
for the Bishop himself, who would not in fact have lived in
the manor. This type of social structure is understandable

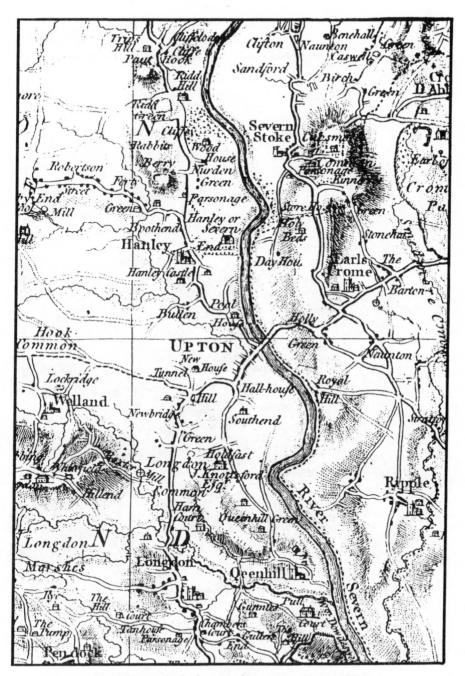

Part of Isaac Taylor's map of Worcestershire in 1772.

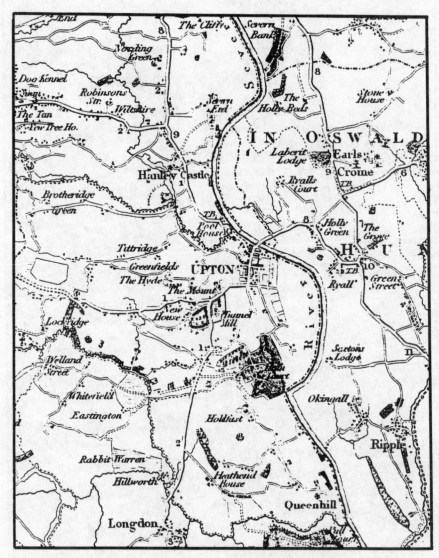

Part of Christopher Greenwood's map of Worcestershire in 1822.

since the area was something of a wilderness where people had to struggle to wrest a living from the soil.

Strangely, the River Severn, which dissected the manor, is not mentioned. One wonders how it was crossed—had there been a ferry at this time one would have expected to find it mentioned, since tolls would have furnished a tidy sum. Since only one mill is mentioned there was presumably some arrangement for transporting corn for grinding across the river. The mill was almost certainly a watermill and there is no indication as to where it might have been.

The woodland was very significant: it had been a most attractive asset to the bishop, who had enjoyed both the hunting and the profits from the timber and honey it afforded. The latter was a very satisfactory bonus in an age when sugar, which now has so large a place in the British diet, was not available. But William the Conqueror changed all that by incorporating into his forest—the great expanse normally called Malvern Chase—the woodland which the bishop had enjoyed in this and neighbouring manors. This made the woodland subject to special laws aimed at protecting and preserving hunting for the king or for any great lord he might choose to appoint lord of the chase. The bishop now had to be content with the lesser, but nevertheless valuable, timber and pannage rights, the latter being the rents charged for allowing pigs to graze.

The last sentence of the Domesday extract indicates that the average income from the manor remained the same in 1086 as it had been 20 years earlier, prior to the Norman conquest. Frequently the value of manors declined, for example, as a result of neglect or even destruction during the unsettled early years of the Conqueror's reign. But Ripple and Upton, unlike neighbouring Hanley Castle, maintained their value. Such stability perhaps reflects a steady and uninterrupted community life.

So far there is little evidence available on which to build up a picture of medieval Upton, but it is possible to trace in broad outline how the parish developed. The registers of the Bishops of Worcester refer to a dispute between the rector of Ripple and the rector of Upton, so it is clear that by the late 13th century—and probably much earlier—each had charge of

his own church, so the parishes had become separated. The
rector of Ripple, which might be called the senior parish, laid
claim to the tithes due from certain 'tenements beyond the
Severn' which, being in Upton, might have been expected to
pay tithes to the rector there. Bishop Godfrey Giffard, no
stranger to quarrels over rights of property, resolved the issue
by awarding the tithes to the rector of Ripple and instructing
him to pay out of them the sum of four silver marks to the
rector of Upton—a neat solution it seems.

By about 1280—the time of the dispute over tithes—77
people were listed as taxpayers in Upton alone, indicating a
substantial increase in population in the two centuries since
Domesday. But the next surviving tax roll, of 1327, lists only
42 names, proving that, even allowing for the numerous
exemptions that were granted, Upton had not escaped the
economic distress and high mortality that had hit the whole
country in the first half of the 14th century.

From this time familiar names start to appear: the tax roll
of 1280 names several people 'de Suthende' (from the
Southend). An inquisition of 1377 refers to Buryfield and to
the often flooded 'Collynghurst', which lay alongside New
Street—like so many New Streets, Upton's is, in fact, of some
antiquity. The researchers for the *Victoria County History*
found accounts of 1479-81 referring to the rent for a garden
'next le gomstoole in Newestretre' which also shows that
Uptonians already had their 'goomstool' or ducking stool for the
punishment of nagging women or dishonest tradesmen. In
1416 a Despencer widow was given as part of her dower (a
widow's portion of her late husband's estate) a third of the
manor of Upton, including burgage rents. Various burgage
rents mentioned in the 15th century add to the evidence that
the town was already a borough, and the layout of the main
streets was probably complete by the middle of this century,
or even earlier. The long narrow plots on which shops were
built enabled a large proportion of shopkeepers to enjoy the
benefit of a frontage on to the main street. A similar policy
was adopted in other towns, such as Ledbury. Another possible
similarity between Upton and Ledbury was the old market
house which by the 18th century was dilapidated and its steps
hazardous. The date of erection of Upton's market house is

not known, but it appears to have been demolished at the end of the 18th century. A great deal of research—both archaeological and documentary—still needs to be done on medieval Upton, but it appears that a market and fair were established in the medieval period, and it is quite possible that the market house was in the High Street near the junction with New Street. The old market cross was probably nearby: it is difficult to pinpoint its original site from which it was moved to spend many years in the grounds of Ham Court, home of the lord of the manor. It has now been incorporated into the war memorial standing in the corner of the old churchyard, a site formerly occupied by two cottages demolished in 1831.

The old market cross in the grounds of Ham Court.

Whilst part of Upton parish was thus developing into a thriving little market town the interests of the 'outparishioners' were more agricultural, a considerable acreage of the parish being farmland. Some of this farmland, in the area called the Hook, lay within the boundaries of Malvern Chase, governed by special laws designed to protect the hunting rights of the king and his favourites. No forest clearance or new building could take place in the Chase except by a special licence, and even farmers in old-established holdings and clearings, made long before William the Conqueror had designated the region as royal forest, worked under difficulty. It was decreed that the deer must be free to wander wherever they chose, and farmers were allowed to erect only low hedges; if the deer leapt or broke through the hedges and caused crop damage the farmers were forbidden to touch them, but had to wait for forest officials to come and drive them off. Forest laws—and they were many and very complex—applied until the 1630s, when Charles I, in an attempt to raise money, disafforested Malvern Chase, thus allowing a considerable amount of development in an area which had, in a sense, been frozen for five and a half centuries. The forest laws, though harsh, were sometimes interpreted leniently, but as late as 1614 two Upton men were indicted at the Quarter Sessions for 'killing a sore deer in the King's Chase called "Malvern Chase"'.

Within the medieval period, then, Upton already showed the diverse character which it has always retained: it fell broadly into two divisions, the one rooted firmly in the soil, and the other centred on the town and commerce, and therefore closely bound up with the opportunities made available by the River Severn which was to medieval people the equivalent of a major railway line or a motorway to later generations.

Chapter II

THE RIVER SEVERN

THE RIVER was of incalculable importance in Upton's development, for it provided employment in fishing, commerce, and all
their associated trades. But it could, and did at times, spell
catastrophe: floods brought distress, while communications
with other towns brought disease, both types of calamity
affecting particularly the crowded alleys that grew up around
Dunn's Lane and New Street. This was the price that had to be
paid for economic opportunities.

From the earliest times fishing was significant in the
economy of riverside communities such as Upton. In 1285
an Act was passed to specify a close season for salmon fishing—
a rather surprising early recognition that there are limits to the
depredations that man can make on his surroundings. Salmon
were a fairly frequent cause of rivalry and ill-feeling between
the communities along the banks of the Severn because it was
possible for those lower downstream to prevent the fish getting
upstream, thereby depriving the fishermen in the higher reaches
of their livelihood. In the Quarter Sessions papers for 1613
there is a petition from hundreds of fishermen in Worcestershire and Shropshire, who claimed that their livelihood was in
jeopardy because the men of Upton, Ripple, Holdfast, and
other villages

> work with forestalling nets which reach from one side of the river
> to the other and from the top to the bottom thereof so that they
> take multitudes of fish namely about 60 salmons at a draught.

The problem was a perennial one, and by 1714 it had become
profitable to catch salmon 'of unsizeable lengths and at
unseasonable times' for sale to fishmongers in London and
other cities—though, given the state of the roads which meant

11

that the journey to London took several days, the condition
of the fish upon arrival probably left a lot to be desired. The
Act making it illegal to take from the Severn, the Wye, and the
Dee any salmon weighing less than six pounds was ignored
like so many others. In 1811, when salmon had reached the
then exorbitant price of three or four shillings (15-20p) a
pound illegal nets were still being seized by the authorities.

Until quite recent times rivers—especially the four great
rivers, the Thames, Severn, Ouse, and Trent—were main
thoroughfares carrying most of the country's trade. Fishing was
one of the activities which presented obstacles to the free
passage of boats, and from at least the 14th century and
possibly earlier Acts were regularly passed forbidding the
building of 'wears, mills, stanks, stakes or kiddles': the frequency
with which the legislation was repeated shows the impunity
with which it was ignored. Certainly Upton had a kiddle—a
net barrier to catch fish—in the 14th century because in a
survey of 1377 the kiddle was said to be in a poor state of
repair and therefore worth only 3s. 4d. Possibly it had been
sabotaged by jealous rivals up-river or deliberately damaged by
Uptonians to comply with the law at the time of the survey.
Of course, it may simply have rotted away.

Other obstacles occurred in the river: an Act of 1543-4
banned the throwing of rubbish and gravel into the Severn so
clearly it was used by some as a convenient rubbish tip. Something quite beyond the control of legislation was the immobili-
sation of river traffic when the river froze over—a phenomenon
encouraged by the design of early bridges which sometimes
impeded the flow of water.

Although in most European countries it was usual to exact
tolls from river traffic this was not allowed on the 'King's
High Stream of Severn' which was described in 1430 as a free
river on which the 'King's liege people' might carry 'all manner
of merchandises and other goods and chattels' without obstruction. But some of the men who lived and worked by the river
had their own way of exacting charges—in 1430 it appears that
'many Welshmen and other persons' attacked the occupants of
boats and destroyed their craft, trying to force them to use the
craft which they themselves hired out. Nevertheless, the Severn
became one of the main thoroughfares, not merely of England,

but of Europe. As early as 1289 the Bishop of Hereford had his wine sent from the port of Bristol up the Severn to Upton, whence it was carried by land to his palace. Other commodities carried at this time probably included salt from Droitwich and the tiles, jugs and other utensils made in nearby Hanley Castle, the centre of a medieval pottery industry. Different ages laid emphasis on different commodities, and by the 19th century the Severn was carrying great quantities of cider, corn and coal. For Upton the river and the quay provided enormous economic opportunities: many of its men were employed on the boats, loading and unloading goods, and escorting cargoes, while others were employed in the various trades which distributed the merchandise or provided services for the people who came to do business in this busy little town. A great deal of Herefordshire's cider reached its final destination via Upton and the Severn—a factor which influenced the development of reasonable roads from Upton to places like Ledbury.

Each river had its own type of craft, and on the Severn the characteristic means of transporting loads was the twin-masted trow which could carry up to 120 tons. A smaller version of the trow was used on the upper reaches of the river where navigation was more difficult, but even these could carry up to 40 tons. The trowmen were skilled in a variety of methods to ply up and down the river: if conditions were right, the wind in the sails carried the vessel along and sometimes it was possible in the lower reaches to drift with the tide, for the Severn is tidal as far as Gloucester. But the trows had to be hauled along many stretches of the river, and this arduous work was done by gangs of men until the 19th century. It was not until 1812 that the horse-towing path was opened for the length of river between Worcester Bridge and the Lower Parting near Gloucester, and as late as 1832 men feared loss of livelihood through the use of horses. According to Turberville, who wrote in 1852 a chronicle of Worcestershire in the 19th century, trade was stopped in 1832

> by the general resistance of the bow-halliers to the use of horses in towing barges up the river. They nailed the gates up along the towing path, and assembled in great numbers to prevent any horses being attached to the vessels. The magistrates made several attempts to convince them of the unreasonableness and folly of their proceedings

but to no purpose. At last the Riot Act was read, and a troop of Scotch Greys marched into Worcester . . . Under this escort the gates were opened and several vessels taken up the river, but not without determined opposition and much disturbance. Eight men were committed for trial to the sessions.

The hauling of vessels was extremely heavy—and very thirsty —work, which helps to explain the profusion of drinking places along the river. The trows themselves could be seen on the river until the present century, but by the later 19th century steam tugs had taken over much of the river transport, and trows have now disappeared almost without trace.

Another, much smaller, characteristic conveyance on the Severn was the coracle, a light and portable means of travel which a man could pick up and carry on his back if his journey involved travelling across land as well as water. Coracles easily capsized, but the men of the Severnside settlements who fished—legally or otherwise—for salmon, eels and other fish were skilful in their operation of this useful little craft.

The advent of the railways caused river traffic to decline. In 1841 the Worcester and Birmingham Canal Company spent £2,000 dredging the river, bringing up 150 tons of gravel daily from the bed of the river. But it presumably had a limited return on its investment. By this time the Bristol and Birmingham Railway line had a station at Defford, only five miles from Upton, and by 1864 Upton had its own station on the Malvern and Tewkesbury line of the Midland Railway. The days of river transport were now numbered.

The Severn brought great commercial advantage to Upton, linking it with towns like Gloucester and Bristol, which was second only to London in importance. But the Severn also presented a practical problem: any traveller by land had to cross it, and for local people it separated Upton from the rest of the original manor of Ripple. Probably there was some kind of river crossing from prehistoric times, and by the Middle Ages there was a ferry. The first bridge was probably built towards the end of the 15th century: the researchers for the *Victoria County History* found mention of a bridge in accounts of 1480-2, with a reference to the ferry, said to be vacant because of the bridge. On other stretches of the Severn ferries continued to operate for a long time. In 1534 an Act was passed

Severn trows, by E. H. Hargrave

forbidding the ferrymen to convey passengers or goods during the hours of darkness—either for safety reasons or to discourage theft.

The original bridge at Upton was wooden. In the 1530s Leland wrote in his Itinerary:

> Upton standith on the right bank of the Severn apon a cluster 4 miles above Theokesbyri, and here is a bridge of wood . . . and here is a great stable of the Kinges a late occupied for great horses, and a nother at Theokesbyri.

The King's stable.

The stable, by the waterside, now shelters a more up-to-date form of transport than the horse—it is a private garage. The wooden bridge naturally needed constant repair, and Hall's Charity was founded partly to provide money for the upkeep of the bridge. Hall's Charity has been the subject of considerable controversy over the centuries. A deed of 1575 specified that the income from certain lands was to be used for three purposes: repair of the parish church; repair of the bridge; and 'other necessary purposes within the parish of Upton'. Such a division of the proceeds of the charity almost inevitably led to arguments about how much might be applied to each purpose and, indeed, what constituted a 'necessary purpose'. It is generally believed that the charity was founded in 1575, but there is much room for doubt about this and about the justification of the very name 'Hall's Charity'. As long ago as 1869 Mrs. Lawson, who wrote the first history of Upton, saw difficulties in the traditional interpretation that Edward Hall founded the charity in 1575, but she did not have access to all the evidence that has since come to light. She noted that the 1575 deed was not a bequest, but a gift made during Edward Hall's lifetime; but she probably had not seen a most interesting document which is now among Upton's manorial records in the County Record Office. This was written by a member of the Bromley family—lords of the manor—apparently at some time in the 18th century. It referred to the lands as having been given

> long before Queen Elizabeth's time tho' the Feoffment of the 18th of Elizabeth (1575-6) is the first I can find of & That is from one Edward Hall to Mr. John Badger, Mr. Edm. Lechmere, ffran. Baker & divers others of Upton & other places.

In the light of this it is reasonable to suggest that Edward Hall was simply a trustee of lands that had been left long before Elizabeth came to the throne in 1558: in 1575 he appears merely to have been passing on—possibly as the last surviving trustee—responsibility to a new body of trustees. A similar confusion, incidentally, wrongly attributed the foundation of Hanley Castle Grammar School to John Knottesford, who passed on trusteeship of school lands in 1585. It is an error that is very easy to make and to understand. Mrs. Lawson thought that an apparently illiterate servant named Edward Hall had figured in the 1575 deed; but the present author has found the inventory made in 1588 of the goods of an Edward Hall of Upton who seems in fact to have been a fairly well-to-do householder, sufficiently affluent to have been suitable to act as a trustee.

Of course, the Bromley document might be at fault, but it does solve the problems posed in the traditional interpretation. Furthermore, there is a certain logic in putting the date of the foundation of the charity before 1530. In that year the Statute of Bridges allowed a county rate to be levied for the upkeep of bridges which were of benefit to all travellers and not simply to the inhabitants of a particular town or parish. Upton's bridge was considered a county bridge rather than a parish one, and it is unlikely that a parochial charity would have been established after the passing of the Statute of Bridges—if someone is already footing the bill there is little point in establishing a new trust to do the same thing. In fact, there were periodic wrangles about who should pay for the bridge, and this smacks of the county trying to avoid the responsibility placed upon it in 1530 and the parish trying to retain as much as possible of the charity for other parochial expenses.

By the 17th century the old wooden bridge was inadequate. In 1605-6 'An Acte for re-edifying of a Bridge over the River of Seaverne neere the Towne of Upton upon Seaverne' was passed. This was an attractive and more substantial structure of red sandstone. Less than fifty years after its completion it fell victim to the Civil War when the arch nearest to the town was deliberately destroyed so that passage was possible only when planks were placed across the gap to provide a somewhat precarious crossing. Even in military terms, the scheme was a disaster because for some reason the planks were left in position so that, in fact, Royalists and Parliamentarians met in Upton: the ensuing battle disturbed the inhabitants of the town, left them a damaged church, and made it clear that even the sacrifice of their bridge had been futile.

After the war the bridge was repaired. According to the Bromley document cited above a meeting was held at the *Talbot* in Worcester to which were summoned, according to the provisions of the Statute of Bridges, the constables and other representatives of parishes in the county. At this meeting it was decided to raise £130 to pay a mason to repair the damage caused in the war, and to appoint two surveyors to keep a check on the state of the bridge.

By the 18th century the bridge was a problem. It was looking very untidy—in 1733 one John Dickins had a pig-sty on it—and the vexed question of its maintenance was becoming more urgent. Whenever the so-called Hall's Charity had been founded it undeniably was partly to help maintain the bridge. But it yielded very little at that time—about £20 a year. Why did the county not pay for the maintenance? As always, no-one wished to increase the rates and the county authorities claimed, with some justification, that the Statute of Bridges had made special provision for the financing of repairs in cases such as this where particular funds, apart from rates, could be applied to bridge repairs. Discussions rather than repairs went on so that by the 19th century the bridge was in a very bad way. It carried a lot of traffic and was also damaged by the habit of mooring vessels to its supporting pillars. In 1814-16, in 1829 and in 1847 the county took legal action against the trustees of Hall's Charity, and considerable sums of money were spent on repairs in 1817 and 1832-4. An offer by the Severn Navigation Improvement group in 1837 to give £5,000 towards building a new bridge was, rather short-sightedly, refused. Endless discussions, reports, proposals and temporary patching up took place in the 1840s. In a sense it comes as a relief to read what T. C. Turberville wrote in 1852.

> the bridge concluded its own history by falling down during a high flood which occurred in February, 1851. It was built in 1605; and there can be no doubt that four of the original arches remained just as they had been first erected, until the day when they tumbled down of sheer old age.

In 1912 the Worcestershire historian, J. W. Willis-Bund, expressed in the *Archaeological Society Journal* his regret

Old Upton bridge, after the floods, in the year 1852.

that the county did not preserve the bridge but built in 1854 'the present most ugly structure'. The 1854 bridge admittedly was scarcely a pretty sight, and, according to Mrs. Lawson, incorporated a drawbridge which in 1883 was replaced by a swing-bridge which cost about £1,500, of which £600 was paid out of Hall's Charity. This was necessary to permit unobstructed passage of boats along the river. By 1912 Willis-Bund was pleased to note that the bridge was thought to be rusting away and had hopes that 'this disfigurement of the river may be done away with'. It is perhaps fortunate that he never saw the modern steel bridge which was built at the start of the Second World War some distance up the river to replace the 1854 bridge. This forced traffic to sweep round the bend into Church Street, thus diverging from the ancient route which had led straight down Old Street and High Street to the river. It finally demolished another tradition too: the romantic may like to imagine Mrs. Lawson's scenes of the old Upton men who congregated on the original stone bridge during all the daylight hours, watching and commenting on the busy life on the river; such romance is unthinkable on today's functional bridge which funnels traffic, blinkered, across the obstruction which the Severn creates in the age of the internal-combustion engine.

Chapter III

TRAVEL BY ROAD

FOR CENTURIES no proper road network existed because it was not necessary. Most communities were reasonably self-sufficient and occasional visits to the nearest market town did not, in the eyes of most people, justify the maintenance of particularly good roads between towns and villages. By the 16th century road maintenance was one of the many responsibilities of each individual parish and the universal attitude was that it was folly to waste time, effort and money providing what was seen as a service for outsiders who were not very welcome anyway. From time to time the county magistrates would try to make parishes fulfil their statutory obligations and in 1633 many Worcestershire parishes, including Upton and its neighbours, were indicted for failing to repair the roads within their boundaries. But such an occasional blitz effected no permanent cure for the appalling state of the roads. Indeed, 'road', which to the modern mind conjures up visions of tarmac and level surfaces, is a flattering term to apply to what was often a wide expanse of trampled mud or a deeply-rutted obstacle course. Despite its position as a market town Upton's inhabitants were no better than anyone else at making the roads safe. Even within the town area, where one might expect the householders and shopkeepers for their own sakes to keep the streets in fairly decent shape, there were traps for the unwary. It was common practice for heaps of rubbish and 'mixons' (dung-heaps) to be left outside front doors, while in 1660 Richard Allies was presented at the manorial court for 'making a sawpit and for laying of timber in the highway'. Even as late as 1827 a young clergyman, Mr. Fothergill, who had taken a service at Longdon and was returning home to

his family at Pool House on the Hanley Road, met his death
when his horse stumbled into a disused sawpit one dark
December night when the road was flooded. His memorial
tablet in Castlemorton church bears a sadly appropriate
quotation from Psalm 69:

> Save me, O God, for the waters are come in, even unto my soul.
> I stick fast in the deep mire, where no ground is; I am come into
> deep waters so that the floods run over me.

Even so, by this time there had been some improvement in
the country's road network for an innovation of the 17th
century proliferated in the 18th to produce what we now think
of as the turnpike era. Many turnpike trusts were formed as a
result of a more widespread desire for travel coupled with the
recognition that the existing system of parochial responsibility
for roads was inadequate. It was laughable to expect that good
roads could be provided by unwilling and unpaid labour using
almost any material that came to hand and supervised by an
equally unwilling and untrained surveyor of the highways—
the important official title of the unfortunate householder
whose turn had come to accept this thankless task. This
amateurish system failed most markedly on main routes, so
turnpike trusts were set up to build and maintain many of
these roads, and levied tolls on the users of them. There was
still a great deal of amateurish incompetence and indifference,
but at last a step had been taken in the right direction for the
trusts, unlike individual parishes, could and often did employ
skilled men who learned from experience and devised improved
methods of road-building.

A turnpike trust based on Upton was founded by an Act
of 1752 to administer the main roads leading from Upton
Bridge to Tirley (now the B4211), towards Colwall and
Ledbury (now the A4104), towards Worcester (now the B4211)
and through Roberts End in Hanley Castle towards Malvern
(now the B4209). As usual the reason given for the foundation
of the trust was the inadequacy of the existing roads which

> are, from the nature of the Soil, and the Narrowness thereof in
> several Places, and by reason of many heavy Carriages frequently
> passing through the same, become so deep and ruinous, that in the
> Winter and rainy Seasons many Parts thereof are impassable for

> Waggons, Carts, and other Wheel Carriages and horses loaden; as also very dangerous for Travellers; and as the same cannot by the ordinary Course and Method appointed by the Laws and Statutes of this Realm now in being, be effectually repaired, amended, enlarged, and made passable, and from time to time kept in good Repair;

The trustees—there were nearly a hundred of them—included members of the local gentry such as William Bromley from Upton, Thomas and John Hornyold and a couple of Lechmeres from Hanley Castle, local clergymen and the leaders of Ledbury and district, too, for the new roads would link up with turnpikes already established and based on Ledbury. This looked very good on paper, the trustees enjoying seeing their names on the official documents and the trust gaining respectability from the influential names apparently fostering it. The reality was a little different for the trustees *were* largely only names, and once the trust was set up the most obvious thing about its meetings was their frequent adjournment: the poor clerk turned up for a meeting almost every week, and time after time—by 1807, for example, on 31 consecutive occasions—had to adjourn because too few trustees attended to constitute a quorum.

The trustees were empowered to erect gates and houses at which tolls would be taken

> before any horse, mare, gelding, mule, Ass, or any other Cattle, Coach, Chariot, Landau, Berlin, Chaise, Calash, Chair, Hearse, Litter, Waggon, Wain, Cart, or any other Carriage whatsoever, shall be permitted to pass.

For each class of vehicle or animal a toll was paid according to a specified scale of charges. The money thus raised was allocated to several purposes: significantly, the first was to defray the cost of getting the Act through Parliament. Secondly it was to provide the cash for the erection of gates and tollhouses, and finally the residue was to be applied to the repair of the roads—an interesting order of priorities. In fact the usual procedure was that the trust borrowed money to pay for all three purposes and the tolls were used to pay the interest on these loans, thus enabling the work to commence, and at the same time offering the affluent middle and upper classes a pretty safe investment for their capital.

Anno Regni vicesimo quinto Georgii II. Regis.

For every Horse or other Cattle, or Beast of Draught, drawing Coach, Chariot, Landau, Berlin, Chaise, Calash, Chair, or other Carriage, (excepting a Waggon, Wain, or Cart) the Sum of Three Pence; for each Horse or other Cattle, or Beast of Draught, so drawing.

For every Waggon, Wain, or Cart, drawn by Five or Six Horses, Mares, Mules, or Geldings, the Sum of One Shilling.

And for every Waggon, Wain, or Cart, drawn by Six or Eight Oxen, or other Horned Beasts only, or by Six Oxen or other Horned Beasts, and One Horse, Mare, Mule, or Gelding, or by Four Oxen or other Horned Beasts, and Two or Three Horses, Mares, Mules, or Geldings, the like Sum of One Shilling.

For every Waggon, Wain, or Cart, drawn by more than Six Horses, Mares, Mules, or Geldings, or Eight Oxen or other Horned Beasts, or by more than Four Oxen or other Horned Beasts, and Three Horses, Mares, Mules, or Geldings, or by more than Six Oxen or other Horned Beasts, and One Horse, Mare, Mule, or Gelding, the Sum of Five Shillings.

For every Waggon, Wain, or Cart, drawn by Two Oxen or other Horned Beasts, and Three Horses, Mares, Mules, or Geldings, the Sum of Eight Pence.

For every Waggon, Wain, or Cart, drawn by Four or any less Number of Horses, or other Cattle or Beasts of Draught, the Sum of Two Pence, for each Horse or other Cattle or Beast of Draught, so drawing.

For every Horse, Mare, Gelding, Mule, Ass, or Beast of Burthen, laden or unladen, and not drawing, the Sum of One Penny.

For every Drove of Oxen, Cows, or Neat Cattle, the Sum of Ten Pence per Score; and so in proportion for any greater or less Number.

For every Drove of Calves, Swine, Sheep, Lambs, or Goats, the Sum of Five Pence per Score; and so in proportion for any greater or less Number.

The tolls specified in the Act establishing the Upton Turnpike Trust in 1752.

The characteristic toll-house is still a familiar landmark, one of the most surprising being the one on the A4104 just above Little Malvern Priory where the alarmingly steep incline must have presented some hazard to travellers, especially in coaches. Tucked in under trees, the road at that point is still not without its difficulties, particularly in winter and in autumn when fallen leaves make the surface slippery. This toll-house, like the ones which used to stand in Upton's New Street, Old Street, Buryfield, and near the top of Tunnel Hill, belonged to the Upton Turnpike Trust. Less noticeable, but more numerous, are the old milestones erected by the turnpike trusts. These may be seen on many old roads, and the A4104 is again a good illustration: several stones are still standing, and two of them gave their names to nearby property—there is a Milestone Farm and a Milestone Cottage. The stones are in varying states of repair though originally it was part of the job of the turnpike surveyor to see that milestones and signposts were regularly painted and maintained. Different turnpike trusts had different styles for their milestones: Upton Trust favoured short stone pillars, about two feet high, sunk into the ground with metal plates fastened to the surface facing the road giving the distance from Upton and to the next town, such as Ledbury.

The toll houses were usually manned by employees paid about nine shillings (45p) a week. The Upton Trust regularly advertised the letting of the gates which meant that an individual would pay the trust a yearly rent for the toll-gate and the right to pocket the takings. In 1804, for example, the Old Street, New Street and Buryfield gates were let to Thomas Watkins for three years at a yearly rent of £268. Such a sum indicates that considerable traffic passed through. The trust, as well as maintaining the road, would keep the houses and gates in repair, but the cost of producing the tickets, paying the gate-keeper and certain other running costs were met by Watkins. The tolls varied according to the degree of damage that particular loads were likely to cause to the road surface so the trust ensured that the weighing machine—there was one in Old Street—was kept in good order.

One wonders how much rivalry there was between the various trusts urging travellers to take a particular route, in much the same way as modern airlines seek to woo passengers

with in-flight films and the like. In 1807 the Upton Trust
resolved that a

Direction post be placed on the side of the road at Little Malvern
where the Worcester Road branches off at that place

to inform travellers that the route to London from Hereford
and Ledbury was about seven miles shorter via Upton and
Pershore than through Malvern.

The turnpike trusts still had to cope with the perennial
hazards like floods and other extremes of climate, as well
as the anti-social habits of people who left their belongings or
rubbish littering the highway—old habits died hard. But the
old haphazard methods of road-building were gradually superseded by more scientific ones. Instead of throwing in a load
of stones and hoping for the best, the trusts employed men
like McAdam, who recognised the need for proper drainage,
firm foundations, and competent surveyors to supervise the
work.

Improvements in roads and better means of travel went
hand-in-hand so the turnpike era was also the era of coaching.
Travelling by coach may, as we look at romantic pictures,
appear very attractive, but in reality it was something of an
endurance test, especially if the weather was bad or one had
the misfortune to be driven by a reckless or unskilled coachman.
Coaches were badly sprung (or not sprung at all) and offered
cramped and poorly ventilated accommodation. Diarists of the
period had little to say in praise of them, grumbling at their
stuffiness, the discomfort, and the irritating or sickening habits
of their fellow passengers with whom they were confined for
long hours, enduring their boring conversations and even, it
was sometimes claimed, acquiring their fleas. Passengers travelling precariously on the roof fared even worse: they were the
first to suffer injury in the catastrophes which occurred when
coaches overturned, shed a wheel, or were simply overloaded,
and it was not unknown for them actually to die from exposure.

The coaches stopped at two inns in Upton, the *Star* and the
White Lion. The latter has become associated with three local
legends. The first is that there was once a fairly famous tomb-
stone in the old churchyard which seems to have aroused the
mirth of earlier generations with its inscription:

> Here lies the landlord of the Lion,
> Who died in lively hopes of Zion;
> His son keeps on the business still,
> Resigned unto the heavenly will.

Secondly, the *White Lion* is reputedly the inn in which Fielding set some of the scenes in his novel *Tom Jones*. Thirdly, the actress Sarah Siddons may have acted in one of the rooms of the inn, but since other places have also been credited with this we may have some reservations about the claim.

In fact, none of these legends is of great importance or interest and the real point about the *White Lion* is its commercial success in the heyday of coaching. Upton was always generously endowed with inns and drinking places, some of which enjoyed a certain notoriety. In 1633 two local farmers of some standing were indicted for 'certain foul and scandalous speeches spoken . . . in an alehouse in Upton', and in 1634 John Browne, who sold ale at all times, and shot a man one night, 'keepeth odious and sinful drunkenness in his house so that his neighbours cannot rest in their houses'. But generally the regular reports made by the parish constables were quite gratifying—the innkeepers sold full quarts of ale for a penny and did not sell during Divine Service or at undue times of the night. They were probably pretty full on the occasion in 1630 when John and Anne Jones with their company of travelling players had provided entertainment including 'tumbling, vaulting, sleight of hand and other such feats' without having a valid licence to do so.

There is a long period about which little is known of the inns and alehouses, but in 1734 the curate, Richard Turberville, throught them too numerous. R. C. Gaut, in his *History of Worcestershire Agriculture* mentions that in the 18th century the *White Lion* was one of the venues for cockfighting in the county. In 1743 it was also the venue for the meeting of the county's parish constables who were to bring with them reports on

> ye state and condition of the roads, highways, hedges, watercourses and bridges within their several parishes.

This, just a few years before the setting up of the Upton Turn-pike Trust, was one of those doomed attempts to get the roads

passable: doubtless the date of the meeting—17 January—
would, being in the middle of winter, add point to what was
required of the constables who struggled to get to the *White
Lion*. To be selected for important county meetings in this
way the *White Lion* must clearly have been the foremost inn
at Upton. Its proprietor in 1804 was probably therefore, like
the turnpike trustees, much put out by the dishonest rumours
spread by

> certain interested innholders who, to serve their own private ends,
> make a practice of falsely representing to their customers that the
> road from Upton to Gloucester is so greatly out of repair as to
> endanger the safety of passengers, and that there are no proper
> accommodations for persons travelling in carriages, either at Upton
> or Corse Lawn.

By 1822, according to *Pigot's Directory*, there were seven-
teen inns and taverns in Upton serving a population of 2,319.
Only the *White Lion* was said to be a posting house. The others
were:

New Street	*The Bell, The Black Boy*
Old Street	*The Cross Keys, The Crown, The Old Crown, The Red Cow, The Seven Stars*
High Street	*The Talbot, The Anchor*
Dunn's Lane (or Queen Street)	*The Black Swan, The Boat, The Severn Trow*
Church Street	*The Wheatsheaf*
Bridge End	*The Nelson, The Star*
Hanley	*The Swan*

Some of these still exist, others are now known by different
names and some, like the *Bell,* are now used as homes or shops.
The last in this list is rather a puzzle—has the *Swan* at Hanley
Swan been included in the list, or does it refer to the *Swan*
on the river front? The *Anchor* was an old-established inn and
figured in a grisly tale of 1831; two bodies, recently buried in
Hanley Castle churchyard, were dug up and sent in packing
cases from the *Anchor* to London. The body-snatchers were
doing a lucrative trade at this time, providing subjects for
dissection at medical schools which were experiencing difficulty
in procuring bodies for use in the training of doctors.

By 1838 the *Star* had joined the *White Lion* in being
advertised as a posting house: the *Prince Albert* coach stopped

here twice daily on its journeys between Malvern and Cheltenham. By 1855 there was a daily service to Worcester from the
Star and the Malvern–Cheltenham coaches now stopped at the
White Lion though only on alternate days. Soon the railways
were to take many of the passengers who had previously used
the coaches and by 1860 the coach proprietors seem to have
decided to make the best of the way things were going: they
laid on daily services to meet the trains of the Great Western
Railway which had built stations at Cheltenham and Tewkesbury. Daily coach services to Malvern and three a week to
Worcester were available, but the extension of the railway
network to include a line and a station in Upton itself in the
1860s dealt the death blow to the coach trade, as it did to river
trade. The railway bridge and station, at the bottom of Tunnel
Hill—a name, incidentally, which pre-dates the railway by many
years—themselves fell into disuse in the 1950s. The station site
is now a local council yard, and newcomers to the town are
scarcely aware that Upton, for nearly a hundred years, offered
freight and passenger services which were of great benefit not
only to the town, but also to neighbouring villages and hamlets,
whose inhabitants came to Upton in a variety of ways—on
foot, on horseback, bicycle and bus. Public transport is now
in decline, and Upton has come to terms with reality, as it has
always done, and offers good parking facilities for visitors
arriving by car to do their shopping or simply to look round
its varied buildings.

Chapter IV

THE CHURCH

THE HISTORY of Upton's churches is not altogether happy. For many years it was a sad chronicle of damage and destruction, minimal repair and short-sighted shoddy building, with periodic frantic attempts to put the place in order. In the shadowy period before the Norman Conquest some place of worship must have existed because we know from the Domesday Book that Ripple and Upton had two priests. Upton's first church may well have been built on the riverside site still occupied by the old tower, and was possibly, like so many churches in a woodland area, a wooden one, which would have long since disappeared without trace. The dispute between the rectors of Ripple and Upton which was mentioned earlier shows that the two parishes became separate at quite an early date. Soon after the dispute Bishop Godfrey Giffard had to intervene again in Upton's affairs by ordering that the infirm rector should be assisted in his duties by Peter de Wye. Clearly the church was very well established in Upton by the end of the 13th century, and in 1297 the rector, John of Monmouth, was instituted as Bishop of Llandaff. A later rector, in 1323, was granted six months' leave of absence 'that he may take over an inheritance newly come to him in Essex'. The newly-appointed Bishop of Worcester, Wolstan, visited both Hanley and Upton in 1339 and dedicated a new altar at Upton. He came again on at least one occasion for an ordination. Upton's familiar landmark—the old tower—dates from about this time so, although evidence is scanty, it seems to have been a period of growth and development in church affairs.

Little has come to light about the church in the later Middle Ages, but an inventory of church goods made in 1552-3 shows that at that time its possessions were modest compared with those of some of its neighbours:

    1 Chalyse the weyte of it xii oz
    a cross of copper gylt
    iii belles
    a broken bell the wyche doth lye in gaze for castyng the other bells
    a blew cope of satan of brydges
    1 sute of blew braunched sylke
    a vestment of tawny velvet
    a vestment of worsted

About this time John Dee was appointed rector, though it is not clear whether he ever actually came to Upton. His early career as a mathematician won him deserved fame and respect: his work on Euclid was important to the history of mathematics in England and he was said to own a most valuable library of 4,000 books and manuscripts, many of them in Greek and Hebrew as well as Latin. None less than Elizabeth I had great faith in him as an astrologer, and she is supposed to have consulted him about the choice of a lucky day for her coronation. By the 1580s, under the influence of the unsavoury Edward Kelly, he became obsessed with spiritualism and they tried many costly experiments to find the mysterious 'elixir vitae' with which to prolong life and turn base metals into gold. By the end of his long life (1527–1608) Dee had aroused much suspicion and resentment, and eventually died in poverty at Mortlake. He maintained towards the end of his life that he was still entitled to the income from the rectory of Upton though he had been deprived of the living during the reign of Mary Tudor when he had been imprisoned for a time on a charge of treason. Incidentally, one of Mary's chief advisers was another local man, Bishop Bonner, who came from Hanley Castle and had been helped in his youth by the Lechmere family.

Upton's parish registers, though dating from 1546, were poorly kept until 1560, and even had parts of pages cut out. No entries were made in 1558—an interesting omission since in that year, according to Valentine Green, who in 1796 published his history of Worcester, 'A sore new sickness raged in Worcestershire, thought to have been the sweating sickness'. Certainly in neighbouring Hanley the death rate was extremely

high that year, which seems to have been marked by a long
hot summer. According to Nash's history of the county, by this
time Upton contained 113 families. As always, the registers
vary in usefulness according to the amount of detail the
incumbents chose to give. There seems to be some disapproval
in the 1586 entry:

> John Gravell of Busheley died sodenly as some suppose with take-
> inge overmuche drincke.

But on the whole the inhabitants of Upton seemed to lead
unremarkable lives.

At the end of the century Richard Eades, playwright and
celebrated preacher, became rector—his family name is still
preserved in the property at the top of Tunnel Hill. He was
chosen as one of the translators of the Authorised Version of
the Bible completed during the reign of James I, but died before
the work started. His probable successor was Miles Smith,
who actually wrote the preface to the translation and eventually
became Bishop of Gloucester.

The first register book was filled by 1627 and the second
volume was beautifully kept until 1646 when the Civil War
caused havoc. From 1624 the rector was William Woodford,
whose appointment to the living had been secured by royal
pressure on the unpopular Bishop Thornborough of Worcester.
Upton had cause to be thankful to James I for his intervention:
Woodford was a kind and dedicated man who served the parish
devotedly for nearly forty troubled years. He resigned his
London benefice and came to Upton—unlike many clergy who
were content to draw the income from their benefices and
delegate the responsibilities to a (frequently ill-paid) curate.
Even when, like so many clergy, he was deprived of his benefice
in the 1640s and replaced by a man more to the taste of the
victorious Parliamentarians, Woodford continued to live in the
district and, taking rather a risk, performed marriages for
certain of his parishioners. During the period of actual fighting
Worcestershire was often in the thick of it. Troops passed
through Upton on several occasions, but the only entries in the
register indicating the state of affairs are in 1644 when 'Jhon
Hasell, slaine by a souldier' was buried in February, and, five
months later 'William Turberville, a souldier' was buried.

1. View from the end of the old bridge in 1886.

2. The 1960 flood – even in recent years Upton has faced this unpleasant threat. Note the railway embankment and bridge abutment, which have now disappeared.

3. & 4. A familiar problem for those wishing to get to Upton in flood-time. The upper picture shows the road from Holly Green on the far side of the Severn. The lower picture shows the road alongside the river bank from Hanley Castle in 1886.

5. & 6.   Floods in New Street, 1924.

7. & 8. Two Upton characters: (*above*) a Severn fisherman, about 1910; (*below*) John Gibbs, local pharmacist and boatowner, braving the floods on his tricycle in 1924.

9. The view from the old bridge, about 1917.

10. This 1970s photograph is taken from about the same position as the last one. The bridge has been demolished, as has the nave of the old church. Note also the disappearance of the tree and its replacement by the war memorial in the corner of the churchyard, slightly left of the centre of the picture.

11. & 12.   The *Swan* – about half a century separates these two views.

13. 'Severn Cottages' in the Hanley Road in the late 19th century.

14. Church Street from the Hanley Road, about 1910, showing the now demolished 'Weighbridge Cottage'.

15.   The swing bridge open.

16.   Operating the swing bridge, *c.*1930.

17. & 18.   The old bridge is replaced by the present one.

19. & 20. The old and new bridges in extremes of climate: (*above*) the frozen Severn, 1891; (*below*) the 1960 flood.

21. & 22. Kent's premises adapted to a more modern trade by the 1930s. Many people called this area 'the Pound'.

23. The Pound in the 1970s.

24. The old churchyard wall before the present bridge was built. The picture shows another of Upton's floods (1924).

25. Church Street, from the Hanley Road, about the turn of the century.

26.   Cramped conditions inside the old church.

27. The old church, about 1910.

28. The old church just before the demolition of the nave in the 1930s. Comparison between this picture and the previous one shows how the church had been allowed to decay.

29. 'Cromwell Cottages', Church Street, before their conversion into a restaurant and chocolatiers. Their name refers to the legend – for which there appears to be no documentary evidence – that Oliver Cromwell spoke with their inhabitants after the 1651 battle of Upton.

30. Soley's Orchard in the 1970s.

31. The present rectory – a lovely building quite overshadowed by the church which was built in its front garden in 1879.

32. A scene from one of Upton's pageants in the 1930s.

However, Upton did not escape the ravages of war, and in 1651, although William Woodford was not officially in possession of the benefice of Upton he was doubtless very grieved by the damage and injury caused when a party of Parliamentarians, having secretly crossed the Severn, used the church as a base from which to fire against Royalist forces attempting to hold Upton. Judge Lechmere of Hanley Castle—the reluctant host of '150 Scottish horse quartered at my House'—noted that in the Upton skirmish there were 'some few of the enemy slaine', though there is no record of their burial in the registers which were not kept from 1648 to 1652.

The confusion in the parish registers in the 1650s—apart from a couple of years when Luke Hackett, the Parliamentarian registrar carefully kept them—reflected the confusion in government. It is with a sense of relief that we find William Woodford back as rector almost as soon as Charles II set foot in England as the restored monarch in 1660. But poor old Mr. Woodford died in 1662 and would have been upset to see the mess made in his carefully-kept register book. After he died Samuel Lynton, who amused himself doodling his name on the cover of the register, was apparently a conscientious curate, while the new rector, Nathaniel Tomkyns, seems to have taken little interest in the parish which he held for nearly twenty years. Francis Phipps, Henry Pantinge, and Richard Smith were the next three rectors. Smith, like William Woodford, stayed in Upton for many years, and in his will left money for the education of poor girls, so he obviously felt real concern for his parishioners.

The church building which had been damaged in 1651 was merely patched up to survive another hundred years. We can get some idea of its appearance from the 17th-century historian, Habington, who, confined to his native Worcestershire for his part in the Gunpowder Plot, spent many years of this pleasant punishment preparing notes for a history of the county. Upton tower, now the only part of the old church still standing, was topped by a spire instead of the present unusual cupola, and there were two chancels, with quite a lot of old and defaced stained glass. The chancel on the left of the altar was said to be the rector's, while that on the right was the parishioners'. Between the two 'under a fayre Arche is a Tombe with a crosse', while under another arch 'curiously wrought with straunge thinges in forren countreyes' there was

> on a raysed monument the portrature of a Knyght and Baron all armed savinge his face, his ryght hand on his swourd threateninge to drawe, on hys leafte arme hys sheylde . . . His legs crossed showethe he was a Knyght of the holy voyage, wch expyred 4 Ed. II., defendinge Christianity against God's enimyes, and at his feate a Lyon. On his right hand lyeth hys wyfe.

This Crusader knight was a member of the Boteler family who held land in Upton, and the monument probably originated in the late 13th or early 14th century. Despite its obvious antiquity it was, as Nash wrote in the late 18th century, 'broke to pieces and used as a foundation stone' when the church was rebuilt in the 1750s. Re-discovered about 1834, this ancient monument was at last accorded renewed respect, and now lies beneath the Roll of Honour in the present church—a much mutilated relic of medieval Upton.

Habington's comments reveal that, even before the Civil War skirmish, the church was not in a particularly good condition. After the war the regular reports made by the churchwardens— churchwardens' presentments—show that there were several reasons for anxiety. There were repeated reports that the church, the parsonage, the bells or the seats were 'out of repair', while in 1687 the churchyard walls

> are now at present part of them fallen downe by reason of this greate flood and we have taken care for the Repairinge of them againe.

Fifty years later the curate, Richard Turberville, criticised the absentee rector, Walter Jones, who had succeeded Richard Smith, and let out the parsonage for an 'annual pecuniary rent', while the state of the parish left much to be desired:

> What a number of Publick Houses are set up in this little town and what Vile Doings are in some of them.

Turberville's letter also contains an interesting social comment on the late 1720s when the death rate soared because

> we had a malignant distemper raging among us, and ye Price of provisions ran very high.

By the middle of the 18th century Upton church must have looked far from picturesque, despite its beautiful spire and prominent position by the river. As we shall see later (Chapter VI), the town itself was dirty and untidy, and the scene by the church can be imagined when we read what the churchwardens reported in 1743:

> Our Churchyards Mound is so low that the swine climb over it, and root among ye Graves. John Willoughby hath a Door opening into ye Churchyard & his family hang old Raggs upon a Line in it. William Pomphrey hath a door opening into the Churchyard, & there are several others that have houses adjoyning & their Chimneys stand upon the Churchyard & the Fishermen lay many of their Fishing Tools in the Churchyard.

In 1749 things were no better, for William Pomphrey and John Willoughby, whose houses probably stood where the war memorial now stands, still had their doors opening into the churchyard and had offended further by using the churchyard to

> lay their ash heaps, hang out their old stockings and other Rags. John Willoughby has cut out a Road for himself and Family to walk in the Churchyard about five foot or two yards broad.

John Benson, who became rector in 1739, had a different sort of grievance:

> Edward Cimmons a Stranger of no good Fame is come into this Parish, & takes upon him to teach ye young people to read, write &c whereas my Curate is much better qualified, would willingly do the same, were he not hinder'd by this wandring Intruder who seldom or never comes to Church, nor goes to any other Place of Worship that I know of.

In December 1754 it was at last resolved to build a new church, and, almost immediately, John Willoughby, possibly the father of the man who had caused all the trouble with his washing and his ash-heaps, was paid to remove the spire from the top of the tower. The tower itself was retained, and during the next two years Willoughby rebuilt the rest of the church for £1,469.

Money was a constant headache. The major cost of rebuilding was met by a levy, the collection of which took the church-wardens ten days, 'being an extraordinary Trouble'. So desperate was the financial position that recourse was made to selling off ancient possessions of the church, including old plate: this was sold for the princely sum of £2 3s. 0d., but 5s. 10d. of the proceeds went, not to the church, but to the cost of hiring a horse to take the plate to Worcester! Four more expensive journeys were made to Worcester 'to try to bargin for a Kings Armes a font a table Iron and marble slab and a branch etc.' Bargain hunting was important—a lot of the stone used was purchased, according to Mrs. Lawson, when the remains of Holy Trinity church in Gloucester were sold off.

By the time that Jonathon Perton had gilded and painted boards with the Lord's Prayer and the ten commandments, the pulpit had been suitably completed and the King's Arms hung resplendently as a finishing touch the neat little church by the river must have looked a pleasing improvement on the sad and damaged building it replaced. Even the churchyard was levelled and tidied up, though the old practice of permitting burial within the church itself—for a fee— seems to have been retained for some years yet. The bells were rung patriotically on occasions such as the allied victories in the Seven Years' War, the capture of Quebec in 1759, and the accession of George III in 1760, as well as for the traditional celebration of the anniversary of the restoration of the monarchy in 1660.

Periodic inspection during the course of construction had always produced from the surveyor complimentary adjectives like 'good', 'workmanlike' and 'substantial', but, nevertheless, there were soon some comments which are sadly familiar. The tower, thought to be quite satisfactory in 1755, was out of repair by 1761, and remained a drain on the finances. Eventually, the man who designed the Infirmary at Worcester— Anthony Keck—produced a design for a lead-covered cupola on top of it, and the clock was replaced. Much worse was to come. Despite the rebuilding of the 1750s, in 1779 the 'whole of the Church Roof being greatly out of repair' meant major expense. Whitewashing the church in 1781, more repairs to the tower in 1793—such things were relatively minor compared with the decision in 1814 to spend no less than £386 on the tower. This time the dome was covered with copper. A few years earlier, probably in 1808, an organ had been installed to replace the older musical instruments like the bassoon.

Foresight, as well as money, seems to have been in short supply. The church was very small, and a gallery, used by the musicians and singers, had been erected at the west end before the church was completed. A second tier of galleries was added in the 1820s when the preaching of the curate, Mr. Furnival, filled the church to overflowing. Anxiety was expressed about the safety of these galleries, but the architects allayed fears with their rather strange report that

> The Fabrick of the Church is not the least injured by them, but on the contrary they act as a support to its walls.

Even John Noake, the 19th-century writer who was keen to preserve all that was good, wrote in his *Rambler in Worcestershire*,

> I cannot speak of this church with any degree of satisfaction.

And, indeed, by this time the church must have looked somewhat peculiar:

> It is in a poor Italian style, with a tower erected on the old walls, surmounted by a cupola which imparts to the whole the semblance of a colossal pepper box . . . There was previously a beautiful spire, which, I am told, far from being badly dilapidated, was pulled down by main force, ropes being tied round it which were pulled by a body of men posted on the other side of the river. The older portion of the tower walls belongs to the Early Decorated period. The church contains two tiers of galleries . . . ranged all round the building except at the eastern end. At the western end is a semicircular recess in the wall, containing a small font, with fixed benches round it, and enclosed with doors which complete the circle. Above this, in the gallery, is a small organ.

The pews, which did not easily permit kneeling, were high and narrow, except for the high square ones provided for the rector and Squire Martin, and some small square ones under the windows. Outside, the churchyard had been extended in the 1820s by the addition of part of the old Horsefair—the area now used as the approach to the modern bridge.

When Victorian piety was at its peak it was recognised that it would be beneficial for the families living at the Hook, about two miles away, to have their own chapel to save them the journey into the parish church. Thus, the Chapel of the Good Shepherd was built and consecrated in 1870: it was designed, like several of Upton's buildings, by G. R. Clarke, whose work included the Upton and Hook schools, and the buildings in the cemetery which dates from 1865. The Hook chapel helped to relieve the pressure on the old church, which had only 506 sittings for a population of over two and a half thousand. One hundred and fourteen of the sittings were in the upper tier of galleries where, as the rector's wife, Mrs. Lawson put it, 'anything like devout worship was almost impossible'.

The Lawsons had a profound effect in the 30 years that Robert Lawson was rector: almost as soon as they arrived in 1864 work started on laying out the cemetery with its two chapels; then Mrs. Lawson wrote the first history of the parish ever published; they steered through the building of the Hook chapel, and next turned their attention to the problems of the parish church itself. The architect, Sir (then Mr.) Arthur Blomfield, drew up plans 'for a handsome church' on the ancient attractive site by the river, but there were objections to disturbing a great number of graves to build new walls. Eventually a completely new church on a fresh site was thought preferable to trying to enlarge and improve the old one. Mr. G. E. Martin, hereditary owner of Ham Court, generously gave as the site the extensive front garden of the lovely house which is now the rectory—though for some years after the church was built the rectory continued to be the old house at the end of Rectory Road. About half of the cost of building the church was met by the Martin family—many people believed that Mrs. Martin was very keen to have the church at this end of town, as she had never liked going from Ham Court through the commercial centre of Upton to worship at the old church. The rest of the money came from Hall's Charity (see Chapter II), the Church-building Societies, and from the dedicated fund-raising of parishioners and their friends.

This new church was consecrated on 3 September 1879 after a farewell service in the old church. Although, like the old church, it was dedicated to Saint Peter and Saint Paul, it was in marked contrast, with its Gothic lines and elegant spire, to the strange mongrel of a building it replaced. The plate, bells and various monuments were taken to the new church, but for the most part it was provided with new furnishings and fixtures which have been added to during its century of existence. As with the Catholic and Baptist churches in Upton, it is best to go and see for oneself what it is like: on every side

The church of St. Peter and St. Paul, consecrated in 1879.

is some reminder, in the form of a gift or a memorial, of old Upton families. The Martins, who, as squires, gave much to both church and parish; numerous rectors, like Richard Smith or Robert Lawson, beloved of their parishioners; soldiers from Upton who gave their lives in World Wars or less spectacular engagements; and the men and women remembered with gratitude as respected doctors, generous benefactors or simply good, kindly souls.

The site of the old church was long neglected, but in recent years—the crumbling nave having been removed shortly before the construction of the modern steel bridge over the Severn—it has been transformed into a somewhat elevated haven in the middle of the chaos of modern traffic. At one end stands the old tower—Upton's quaint pepperpot landmark—and at the other end is the war memorial erected like so many others in that shocked but hopeful period after the First World War. This historic site is the very heart of Upton: it saw not only its religious origins, but lay next to its commercial centre and the river. Currently (1979) it is being suggested that the tower might well become a heritage centre for Upton, and, whatever practical problems might lie in the path of that scheme, there could scarcely be a more suitable home for a heritage centre. The site and the stonework on it have witnessed so much that is important to Upton that it is a most remarkable inheritance.

Chapter V

DISSENT IN UPTON

ALTHOUGH THE LAST four hundred years have seen gulfs between the various denominations they share a common heritage since throughout the Middle Ages to be a Christian in western Europe was to be a Roman Catholic. The Tudor monarchs repudiated the authority of the Pope and put themselves at the head of the Church of England, but until this time in the 16th century the people worshipping in the old church by the riverside were Catholics. Many people rejected the Tudor religious settlement, for, although it was assumed that a ruler could dictate the faith of his subjects, there was a growing feeling that a man's religion and conscience were his own affair. Even Elizabeth I—never one lightly to throw away her rights—is supposed to have claimed that she had no wish to make 'windows in men's souls'. Nevertheless, those who rejected her religious settlement risked fines, social isolation, and, in some cases, even torture and death, when it was suspected that their religion undermined their loyalty to their monarch. Some of these dissenters would not renounce the doctrines and authority of the Pope, while others, keen to give up these things, felt that the changes made by the Church of England had not gone far enough. Despite her desire to pursue a 'middle way' Elizabeth was unable to please everyone.

In Worcestershire there was always strong support for the Roman Catholic tradition, and, next door to Upton, the rich and influential Hornyold family became its champions in Hanley Castle. It seems to have been less strong in Upton though Mrs. Lawson claims that it was the Hill family's continued support of the old faith that led to the curious entry in the burial register of 1583:

41

Roger hill died the xxiijth daie of June and was brought to the
Churche to bee buried, Butt the Curatt for divers causes refused to
bury him.

Evidence is very scanty, and by the mid-17th century there
were said to be no Papists, but there are occasional references
in the churchwardens' presentments to persons suspected of
being Papists. One such was Elizabeth Parsons in 1676, though,
as if excusing her, it was added that she was 'but a poor person'.
Much of the hostility felt towards Catholics was due to fear
that they might topple the government, for they acknowledged
as their head the Pope, who wielded considerable political
power. The belief that Catholics were traitors was encouraged
by events like the Gunpowder Plot in 1605, and the autocratic
habits of Stuart monarchs like Charles I and James II—suspected
or proven Catholics—did not enhance the picture that many
people had of Catholicism. In the minds of many, and not
without some justification in the tortured 17th century,
Catholicism and trouble went hand-in-hand. Unfortunately,
the suspicion lasted long after Catholics had ceased to be a
threat to the established church and to the constitutional
monarchy which developed under William and Mary and their
successors. Throughout the 18th century certain professions
like teaching were forbidden to Catholics, and so, too, were
positions of public or military authority. Although they
gradually won the right to worship unmolested in their own
way they did not achieve full civil rights in England until
1829. There is an oral tradition that during this difficult time
Upton had a small Catholic community which worshipped
at first somewhere in Buryfield, and later in a room near the
Crown in Old Street. This has yet to be conclusively proved,
but certainly in 1749 the churchwardens reported four people
said to 'have embraced Popery' and the survey made of the
bishopric of Worcester between 1782 and 1808 states that
there were four Papist families here.

After 1829 things became much better for the Catholics—
indeed, by 1841 Thomas Charles Hornyold of Blackmore
Park in neighbouring Hanley was appointed the first Catholic
High Sheriff of Worcestershire, having already made history
as one of the first Catholic magistrates in England. His family
was responsible for building the Catholic church and a small

Catholic school in Hanley Swan and, not long after, in 1849, land was purchased to build in Upton the Catholic church dedicated to St. Joseph and opened in 1850. The Upton church, in local red brick, was a much more modest affair than the more flamboyant edifice at Hanley Swan, though both were designed by Charles Hansom, brother of the man who designed the Hansom cab. Both churches were served by priests of the Redemptorist order: their missionary zeal had brought them from their native Belgium to win converts in the rural parishes of England. They had a small monastery at Hanley and a priest from this monastery served Upton for some years. At about the same time a school for about sixty Catholics was kept by a young man called Reuben Stockall, who lodged for a time in Old Street with the family of James Lyse, the carrier to Worcester. The school, according to the 1855 *Billings' Directory,* was 'situate by the Severn side', but it is possible that it was just a Sunday school.

After some years the Redemptorists left Hanley, and Upton has since had a succession of priests living in the presbytery adjoining St. Joseph's church in School Lane. For many years the Upton priest also ministered in Pershore until, in 1943, the Pershore community was given its own resident priest. This was during the long ministry of Father Wharton who worked in Upton from 1929 to 1961. He was a leading figure in the organisation of events like the fetes and pageants of 1933 and 1934, and was for many years a parish councillor. He had a tradition of flying appropriate flags in the presbytery garden on days of public celebration—the White Ensign would be seen fluttering on Trafalgar Day, the Union Jack on royal occasions, and so on.

The church and presbytery have undergone some changes over the years, but they have been small compared with the changes in attitudes. Catholics no longer have to practise their religion in secret, and, though their number is small, they have managed to survive against great odds.

Whilst the Catholics were at one end of the religious spectrum, at the other end were those who wanted much more far-reaching changes than the Church of England had adopted. Like the Catholics, these Protestant nonconformists were regarded with suspicion and suffered for their beliefs.

It is extremely difficult to be precise about when Protestant
dissent started in Upton, but, since Upton was a commercial
centre in direct contact with other towns along the Severn, it
is quite likely that it was exposed at an early date to ideas
which took longer to reach more remote rural areas. As early
as 1598 certain children were buried without having been
baptised. This may possibly point to their being the offspring
of dissenters who did not believe in infant baptism. Herbert
Cox, minister of the Baptist church in the 1950s, put the
foundation date at 1653 when Richard Harrison of Dymock
is said to have led the congregation worshipping in a house
in Dunn's Lane—probably number eleven. This is in agreement
with the popular belief that the church was founded quite soon
after the Parliamentarians had been in the town for the battle
of Upton, but there is as yet no documentary evidence for
this date. In 1662 the church authorities were assured by the
churchwardens that there were 'noe papists, annabaptists . . .
Quakers or other separatists' in the parish, although several
persons were reported for failing to attend church—sometimes
a way of insinuating that their religious beliefs might be alien
to the established church. Mrs. Lawson and her contemporaries
put the foundation of the Baptist church at about 1670 and
this does, on the evidence so far amassed, seem reasonable.
In 1669 John Baylis was reported 'for keeping a conventicle
in his house upon a Sabath Day', and one wonders if his house
was the place in Dunn's Lane traditionally thought to have
accommodated the Baptist church. There is another piece
of evidence that the Baptist movement was well established
in the late 17th century: a churchwardens' presentment which
appears to date from 1682 laments:

> And I would wish wt all my soul yt in ys we had not one schisma-
> ticke refusing communion wt ye church of England to present, but
> behold a whole troup, all anabaptists.

And also, four women

> after delivery from ye perill of childbirth refused to make their
> publicke thanksgiving to god in ye church.

Prejudice against the Protestant dissenters led to some ugly
scenes despite the fact that after 1689 they were supposed to
enjoy freedom of worship. Sometime in the latter part of

the reign of Queen Anne (1702–14) William Hankins, who had come about 1693 to live in Upton as resident Baptist minister, had to beat a hasty retreat from a service.

> A mob of High Church Furies came one Lord's Day to take Mr. Hankins and disperse the Society; the brethren were apprised and fastened the door, the mob attempted to force it open, and actually thrust an iron bar through it . . . then attempted to hew the door to pieces. The back part of the house being near the River gave an opportunity to Mr. Hankins to escape in a boat out of their hands.

This account comes from the record of Samuel Trevor in the late 18th century and adds weight to the notion that the meeting house was in Dunn's Lane, thus having rear access to the Severn. However, by the time Trevor was writing the Baptist community had built the church which still stands in Old Street. This dates from 1734 and the Manse was built soon after. The church records are a little misleading, because somehow the building licence was mislaid and a new one was sought in 1793—but the building itself dates from 1734. At the back of the church was a burial ground which has now been made into part of the Manse garden.

By the end of the 18th century the Methodists, too, had gained ground in Upton, and John Wesley himself came to preach in 1770 in the newly-built Wesleyan chapel. This still stands at the left-hand side of the Co-operative Society's car park in Court Street at the back of the grocery stores. Later there was a chapel in the Walk, which runs alongside the present Anglican church, but in 1891, soon after that church was built, the Wesleyans opened a new chapel at the bottom of New Street. It was a short-lived scheme and was converted for secular use within about twenty years: it is now Shipp's Garage.

Meanwhile, the Baptists continued to prosper, despite John Noake's comment in his *Rambler in Worcestershire* (1851):

> There are Baptist and Wesleyan Chapels in the town, but Dissent does not seem to be in a flourishing condition here.

According to Bishop Hurd's survey of the diocese of Worcester, 1782–1808, the Protestant dissenters in Upton were much more numerous than the Catholics, having 18 families of adherents to the Catholics' four. In 1850, a couple of months after Upton's Catholic church was opened, Alexander Pitt, the

Baptist minister, joined in the debate at the Shire Hall to condemn 'papal aggression'—Catholic dioceses had just been set up in England—and religious feeling ran very high. The Baptist church and adjoining schoolroom were both enlarged in 1863–4. The schoolroom still serves the Sunday school and is also used for meetings of certain societies and committees in the town. The church itself, despite its austere exterior, is internally welcoming, and by the communion table are the lovely carved chairs believed to date from the 17th century when the Baptists were still struggling for existence. They have come a long way since then, and the minute books show that the struggle did not end even when the law of the land gave them liberty of worship. Every member of the church was required to live a pious and upright life after adult baptism and acceptance into the church. Failure to attend Sabbath meetings regularly would result in dismissal from the church, and the slightest moral failing could lead, not only to exclusion from the fellowship of the church, but to public denunciation and disgrace. No kind of ecumenical feeling existed in the 18th and 19th centuries, and the slightest inclination to anything remotely like 'Romish practices' was stamped upon instantly. Even the Pastor was not above criticism and was urged to depart if he was found lacking in the least respect.

Today Upton has places of worship for three denominations —Anglican, Baptist, and Roman Catholic, and, happily, the old days of fierce antagonism are gone. All three have their origins in the riverside site by the old tower.

Chapter VI

LAW AND ORDER IN THE MANOR OF UPTON

SOME RECORDS still exist of the proceedings of the manorial courts held regularly in Upton. The manorial courtroom was not the building at the junction of School Lane and Court Street—this area derived its name from much later developments in the 19th century. The old manorial court was probably in Church Street, opposite the tower of the old church, and part of the property of the lord of the manor, in whose name was summoned the court baron for the enforcing of manorial customs and the court leet for dealing with petty offences.

Ownership of the various manors in Upton in medieval times is very complicated and scarcely worth trying to pursue in great detail here. The manors fell to a succession of lords from different families: the bishops of Worcester figured large in early times and a succession of Saltmarsh, Boteler and Despencer families staked their claims against lesser known rivals. Later on the Earls of Warwick took possession until Henry VII confiscated all the estates of the young earl, whose chief offence was to have a stronger hereditary claim to the throne than Henry himself, who had won it on the battlefield at Bosworth. Other men—Compton, Bourne and Croft—held the central manor of Upton briefly during the early Tudor period until at last stability was achieved when Henry Bromley bought it in the 1590s. Direct succession from father to son kept the manor in the Bromley family until 1756, when William Bromley's daughter Judith inherited. Through her marriage into the Martin family stability was maintained because the Martins held the estate right through to the present century, living at Ham Court, the house built by Judith and John Martin on the old site a mile or so south from the town centre. Ham

47

Sir Henry Bromley, aged 27. A.D. 1587.

Sir Henry Bromley, first of the Bromley lords of the manor of Upton.

was the old term for good summer pasture land and Ham Court was built above the flood level of Upton's ham.

But the Bromleys, and later the Martins, owned much property in the centre of the town as well, and it was probably in the town that the manorial courts were held. Manor officials —the aletasters, the tithingmen or constables—were appointed at these courts until well into the 18th century, and various offenders were presented to the steward of the court. Some of the evidence laid before him in the 17th and 18th centuries paints a vivid picture of the small market town and quickly dispels any romantic visions of a quiet town where homes and shops were kept spotless by jovial occupants unharassed by the pressures of modern life. Upton was crowded, smelly and untidy, bustling with the activity which had long been part of its tradition as a medieval market town and borough. As well as the weekly Thursday market there were fairs four times a year for the sale of cattle, sheep and horses: the old Horsefair site is now the approach to the modern bridge. A mop, at which farm labourers were hired, was also held from time to time, attracting farmers from many of the neighbouring villages, and men and women, often from quite far afield, seeking work as shepherds, milkmaids, fieldworkers, and so on.

In the centre of the town was the High Street which is probably where the old market house stood. It seems to have resembled the one still standing in Ledbury: a raised stone area, approached by steps and surmounted by a large meeting room supported by pillars. Unfortunately, nothing now remains of it, and even people who have known Upton all their lives have been surprised to learn that it still existed in the 18th century, as no tradition of it seems to have been passed down from preceding generations. In 1719 the 'Market house and steps leading thereto' were 'very much out of repair' and it seems quite likely that it was demolished in the later 18th century— possibly to make the main street more easily negotiable by the coaches that had started to create traffic problems. There was an area beneath the market house where traders were tempted to set up stalls and display their wares, though this was for- bidden. In 1660 Ralph Jackson was threatened with a fine of 39s. 11d. 'for keeping a stall within the compasse of the

Ham Court, the seat of John Martin.

markett house'. Presumably the fine with which he was threatened was so high because he had repeatedly offended in this way.

Many orders were passed to try to prevent anyone establishing any right to practise his trade in the area of the market house. But it was very natural for traders to try to set themselves up in this choice spot to attract trade from passers by, and the frequency with which such orders were renewed shows how often they were ignored. In 1660:

> It is ordered that no persons shall place or lay any Cariots Cabiges or turneeps w'thin the compasse of the markett house.

> We doe order that no person whatsover shall pitch or sett up any stall or standing w'thin the sayd markett house or sweale any hoggs or hang any leather.

The orders of 1690 forbade some other nasty customs which destroy any illusion that Upton was a picturesque little town and help to explain why Upton, like many other places, was visited by the plague in 1665.

> wee do order yt no person shall suffer any pigg or piggs about the Towne to go unringed

> wee do order yt no Cowes Bellys be emptied in the streetes by ye buchers

> wee do order yt no person within ye Berrow (borough) shall suffer any Mixon (dung-heap) to lye before his dore above the space of 16 days

To let one's dung-heap lie outside the front door for up to 16 days (in 1660 the limit had been 14 days) was presumably quite acceptable. The order simply made it clear that the thing should not be left indefinitely, growing to ever greater dimensions and making the road impassable. Indeed, passage was quite difficult at any time since everybody did just what he liked in the road until it was made plain to him that he could not. In 1660 Edward Allies had made a sawpit, and, like Edward Baylis, left timber in the highway. Many years later, in 1733, John Dickins showed enterprise and little concern for the general public when he built a pig-sty on the bridge, presumably using the conveniently-shaped passing bays which were let into

The ducking stool.

the walls to enable pedestrians to avoid injury as heavily-laded beasts and cumbersome wagons and coaches passed over the narrow bridge. There were also complaints in 1758 about

> all Coal Owners that fills the Quay with Coales and Slack to stand hindering other business

while there was still the old grievance against

> all persons that lodges timber in the Horsefair longer than one month.

It was directed in 1758 that any fines collected were to be given to the poor. But, quite apart from fines, the town possessed three other typical means of punishment: a whipping post, stocks, and a ducking stool. The ducking stool, often called a goom-stool, was the means by which a male-dominated society took its revenge on sharp-tongued female troublemakers and, occasionally, dishonest tradesmen. The victim was strapped to the stool and lowered into the evil-smelling waters of the lake at the bottom of New Street. It was a fearsome punishment: the fact that in 1690 it was forbidden to 'throw any Carron into ye gum stoole lake or into ye ditch belonging to Collinghurst' is a pretty certain indication that it was common practice to dispose of all kinds of rubbish in this way. During the period 1673 to 1758 fairly frequent reference is made to the stocks and whipping post, which generally seem to have been kept in good repair. But, happily one might think, the ducking stool, sometimes also referred to as the cucking stool, was often in need of repair or apparently missing altogether.

The whole New Street area seems to have been best avoided altogether if possible. In October 1690 Zachariah Stoakes was presented

> for not clensing the ditch at ye gum stole: which is ye occassion of ye watters lying in ye high way. which prevents peoples going to, and from, the towne.

But apparently it was not expected that he would hurry himself to put matters right—he was to be fined if the ditch was not cleaned out by the following March, it not being clear just how people would manage during the winter months. At the same time James Chamflower was brought before the court for

> a breach of a former order for stoping up ye driftway in a floud
> time out of Collinghurst into ye new Streete.

Blocking the driftway when people were trying to rescue
their livestock from the all too common floods obviously made
the offender unpopular. Incidentally, the parish register indicates
that a few years later New Street was hit by a different sort
of disaster:

> A Fire brake out in Robert Hazels workhouse in ye New Street
> July the 6th 1705 which burnt down ye workhouse & Barn and
> ye Parish house in which Barthol. Pumpfry dwelt. praised be God
> that it burnt noe more.

In 1728 the surveyors of the highways—who should have
been setting a good example—were presented 'for not repareing
the causeway under the churchyard wall' and two men were
in trouble

> for stoping the watercourse against the churchyard and for not
> remouveing their soyle which is a common annusance in the
> highway.

There were usually other 'common annusances' too: several
people failed to keep their 'convenient house' in order, while
one man kept 'an unlawfull dog wh fell upon one Leonard
Jones and hurt him very sore'. In 1660 Thomas Browne, one
of several presented for 'laying of hillucks in the street', faced
quite a list of charges: he sold ale 'by unlawful measure' and
also brought

> a diseased horse in the Towne of his owne accord, to the great
> annusance of the people in our towne which horse died in his
> stable.

Thomas Browne also brought in two other unwelcome
visitors: 'John Huntly and one taylor a hotwater man w'thout
giving of security'. This was a matter about which the parish
was constantly vigilant for strangers might become a charge
on the poor rates (see Chapter VII) so various people were
presented for harbouring strangers.

Other snippets from the manorial presentments, though not
particularly important in themselves, make interesting contributions to a general picture of Upton and its inhabitants.

Soley's Orchard, Rectory Road.

This was one of the homes of the infamous Captain Bound, whose ghost was said to have ridden about Rectory Road and the Southend for many years—supposedly unable to rest because of the captain's sinful life and mistreatment of his successive wives. One of Upton's legendary characters, the poor man probably did little to earn such an evil reputation!

The town seems usually to have been gratifyingly free from 'nightwalkers and eavesdroppers', though two women were presented as such in 1725. Similarly, violence was rarely mentioned, though a man, later described by the churchwardens as 'scandalous' in his life, was presented

> for bloudsheds uppon Richard gurney—constable and uppon Thomas Parsons at the same time.

Then there was the man presented

> for not bringing the towne weights to light and we doe order that he shall make them good by all saints day next:

When Charles II was succeeded by his Catholic brother James the rebellion led by his illegitimate son, the Duke of Monmouth, was put down savagely: a whiff of the national unease at the time might be detected in the stout claim of 1685 that in Upton

> we have not any that hath committed any murder or fellony or Treason against the King or this present government to the best of our knowledge.

Those who dwelt in the more rural parts of the parish were angry when they saw the cattle of people who lived in neighbouring parishes wandering—or being driven—on to the common or wasteland of Upton to consume the grass that should have been nourishing Upton's beasts, so there are several references to this in the manorial records. More unusual is the presentment of poor Widow Lingham in 1730 'for letting Two bay of buildings fall'. Given the overall picture of Upton, the resultant mess probably did not look too much out of place, being just another of the 'annusances' to be avoided by the luckless walker.

In 1684 a brickmaker called Edward Addis made an agreement with Henry Bromley which for a long time must have rendered unsightly the stretch of river bank between Upton Bridge and the less important bridge which crossed the stream known as Poolbrook. Addis was permitted to dig out clay by the side of the river and set up his kilns and piles of bricks in part of the nearby Horsefair, provided he left 'sufficient roome for all manner of Carriages to pass without danger' and also agreed to sell his bricks to anyone in Upton for ten shillings (50p) a thousand—except Henry Bromley who was to have them cut-price at nine shillings. In view of this agreement it comes not altogether as a surprise to find that in 1716 it was quite rightly suggested that digging holes in the Horsefair was 'dangerous and ought to be presented'.

The traditional manorial courts which were a legacy of the Middle Ages ceased to be held in Upton a long time ago, though exactly when is not yet clear. Such courts have never been formally abolished, but since they are now most unusual and since Upton no longer has a traditional lord of the manor it is not likely that it will ever see such a regular practice revived. The courts now held in Upton deal with offenders against the law of the land rather than manorial matters.

Chapter VII

THE POOR

TODAY WE DEMAND a much higher standard of living than any earlier generation, and it is difficult to conceive of the grinding poverty that existed in places like the overcrowded and insanitary alleys close to the river in Upton. Conditions were less crowded, but scarcely more pleasant, in some of the hovels occupied by the poor in the more outlying rural parts of the parish. From Elizabethan times each parish was responsible for caring for the poor within its boundaries, the unenviable task of supervising poor relief falling to the unfortunate householders whose turn had come to serve for a year as unpaid overseer of the poor.

Those requiring relief had to apply to the overseers and anything they received was a grant, not a right, made out of the proceeds of the poor rates levied on all property in the parish. The rates were collected as well as distributed by the overseers who had to account to the ratepayers for every penny. Occasionally they were called to heel for undue generosity or too great an intake of liquid refreshment at the sometimes lengthy parish meetings. In Upton this happened, for example, in 1712, when the cost of poor relief had rocketed up to twice the amount spent in previous years. Another concern was that the parish should foot the bill only for its own inhabitants so newcomers were regarded with suspicion and were likely to be hustled quickly away unless they could produce a settlement certificate by which the parish of their origin acknowledged them and agreed to pay any expenses should they become in need of poor relief. From time to time some kind of investigation took place in order to ascertain how many 'foreigners' had contrived to settle in Upton:

58

1707 Spent with the churchwardens in consulting about several which are intruded into our parish.

1724 Paid for a warrant to bring in severall Persons to proove their parish and examination.

1770 Ordered that the Officers do take the following persons to be examined touching their settlements and remove them soon as possible to their respective parishes.

When people were removed to their place of settlement they were given a pass by the local magistrates. Their journey was supervised by the constable of each parish through which they passed, and he, or the churchwardens or overseers, often granted them a few pence to buy food to sustain themselves on the wearisome walk. Since it was believed to be a crime to ask for help from a 'foreign' parish some constables saw fit to administer a whipping at the whipping post, which in Upton was kept in good repair. Similar passes were issued to discharged soldiers or sailors, and all added to the cost of poor relief in the parishes through which the holders travelled.

Pregnant women—especially if they had no husband to support them—were rushed out of a strange parish as rapidly as possible unless they could prove a settlement. They were too expensive to be welcome: they had a habit of needing medical attention and might well leave a helpless infant on the hands of the parish officials, while if they died there was a funeral to be paid for. Upton's overseers actually rewarded the vigilant who reported pregnant women who arrived in the parish:

1720 Tho. Prichard a qt of ale for giveing an acct of a bigg bellied woman - 3d.

Sometimes a woman would be paid to go away:

1707 Spent upon a strange woman bigg with childe & in devouring to pass her by us - 5s. 6d.

1718 to a great bellied woman to send her away - 9d.

For Upton's own inhabitants the grants made by the overseers took various forms. Sometimes a more or less regular weekly allowance was made, as in the case of widows struggling to bring up a young family. Sometimes a family's rent was paid: this was normally paid quarterly or half-yearly and the

£2 or £5 required was beyond the pocket of a labourer whose wages of a few shillings a week barely covered the cost of food. Sometimes the grant took the form of clothing, coal or some out-of-the-ordinary requirements like medicine or white bread for an invalid. The following are typical examples from the overseers' accounts, the first example being taken from one of the most insensitive periods of poor law history when the poor who received parish help were obliged to display a large 'P' on their clothing to denote their pauper status.

> 1705   for sowing on the Badge - 3s. 0d.
> 1708   Gave William Peny his wife haveing the small pox - 1s. 6d.
> 1709   Roger Edgin in Bread and burly to sow his garden - 2s. 2d.
> 1711   bread and drink at Hannah Niblett's child's funerall - 2s. 6d.
> for laying out ye child - 6d.
> Hannah Niblett's child's coffin - 2s. 6d.
> 1714   To Bess Griffin her children being sick with the small pox
> 4s. 6d.
> To ye Widd. Bishop being sick with ye small pox - 2s. 6d.
> To Pumphery for Burying ye Wid. Bishop - 2s. 0d.
> For bred ys week for Bishops family - 4s. 6d.

Although these entries are in themselves typical they have been selected because several of them involve some particularly unfortunate families. Life was very much a gamble in the days before health or unemployment insurance—Hardy's Mayor of Casterbridge who rose to the heights of parochial power and plummeted to the depths of poverty was not entirely a figment of the author's imagination. A cruel twist of fate could reduce anyone to a desperate plight, and the account books show that the overseers took great trouble over some of the families mentioned above. William Peny was given almost daily help in the critical winter of 1708 when his wife was so ill with smallpox: money, blankets, bread, meat, drink, candles, oatmeal, salt and a bushel of corn were granted with remarkable generosity. Widow Bishop's family was cared for after her death from smallpox; her numerous children were kitted out with new clothes and even her pig was seen to, being brought into town, presumably for sale—unless the animal was to be added to the considerable number allowed to wander all over the place foraging for food. Bess Griffin was a perennial problem with her illegitimate children. In

1714 it cost over a pound to send her to jail and get her out again, though probably her only crime was refusal to name the father of the latest addition to her family, for the church-wardens reported to the church authorities in July that she had had a child and the father was unknown. Roger Edgin's family suffered insurmountable problems: two children were buried in 1712, and his wife, who had helped to nurse a sick woman, died herself in February 1713. The woman Roger Edgin sub-sequently married seems to have become insane in later life and the parish cared for her as well as was possible in an age which knew nothing about mental disorder.

For the most part, the poor rates provided basic essentials for people who were in financial difficulties or too sick or aged to work. The system was very flexible and worked reasonably well in a small community where the most useful means of helping—whether it was cash, a new smock, medicine or whatever—was usually quite obvious to the poor law officials, who were also neighbours. Abuse of the system by the profes-sional layabout was not common. There was a social stigma attached to 'going on the parish' and, since one's circumstances were usually public knowledge, attempts to deceive the parish officers were likely to receive short shrift. Most relief was 'outdoor relief', meaning that it was given to people living at home rather than in a workhouse or poor house. Many homes were grossly overcrowded by modern standards, and sometimes it seems that they were considered so even by contemporary ones:

> 1762 At a parish meeting it is ordered that the Overseer doe turn out of the House where Wm. Grimet and Wm Jefferis doe now live one Martha Cope and Wm. Grimet's oldest children who are cappable to Gett their Liveing in order to make Roome for ye said Wm. Jefferis and his small children who complain for want of Roome in the sd. House.

This refers to one of the houses owned by the parish, but it is not clear where it was. Some parish houses provided homes for one or two families, while others were more in the nature of a poorhouse that was used to accommodate the impotent poor who could not earn a living at all. As far as possible the poor were made self-sufficient and this was carried even to the extent in 1774 of paying 8s. 8d. 'to Watch a Man at the

Wheatsheaf to Prevent his leaving his Wife'. But it does seem that there was a poorhouse in Upton: in 1724, 1s. 4d. was paid for 'halling Thomas Jones' goods to the parish house' which probably meant that Thomas Jones had become unable to support himself so was received, with all his possessions, into the shelter of the poorhouse.

The able-bodied poor were often put into a workhouse where they had to pay for their keep by working long hours at boring tasks. It is not yet clear when Upton had its first workhouse, but there was certainly one in the 1760s.

In 1763 the parish purchased from the Martin family a house in the pig market and modified it to become a new workhouse. It was probably the old building which stands in Court Street (as it is now known) and lies next to the yard behind the *Talbot Head*. Its first master was John Palfrey who seemed often to fall out with the parish officials about the financial arrangements. He and his wife were allowed the customary accommodation plus their wages of five shillings (25p) a week, and in 1767 there is a terse little entry that he should be allowed in addition 'half a pound of butter and no other perquisites'. The parish paid out substantial sums to Butcher Morris and Baker Shipman so it would seem that, at least initially, the poor were well catered for, though the children probably had mixed feelings about the few pence spent on their 'treakle and brimston'. We find, for example:

			£	s.	d.
December 14th 1764	155lbs. Beef	..	1	9	7
	117¾lbs. cheese	..	1	9	5
	Sugar and Plumbs at Christmas	..		1	6½
January 3rd 1765	9lbs. Beef	..		18	11½

It therefore comes as something of a surprise to read that in 1776 it was ordered

> that all the Paupers in the Workhouses shall have a dinner of fresh provisions at least once a week and that upon a Sunday.

By this time John Palfrey had left—there had been some dissension in 1774 over his wages—and John Stott was master at £21 a year. He was required not simply to administer the workhouse but

as well to instruct each individual that shall be in the workhouse at
any time who is capable of it, in the woollen industry.

This probably meant that he was to teach them to spin, for
it had been resolved in 1774 'to Establish the Spinning trade
in the Workhouse'. A later master, William Waring, was probably a weaver so he perhaps taught weaving to the inmates. On
the whole, the work done in the workhouse seems to have been
boring and repetitious, and to have included that traditional
occupation for paupers—oakum picking. This was one of the
most tedious tasks ever devised, but doubtless it was in demand
in a riverside community. It involved picking old lengths of
rope to pieces to provide the fibre used in boat-building to
plug the seams before the whole structure was tarred to render
it waterproof. The more skilled operations in boat-building
were not done by paupers—they merely did the menial task
that provided a cheap raw material. Some further indication
of the frustrations of workhouse life is given in 1767 when it
was decided to

find a Block and materials for pounding hemp in the House to
employ the able youth and likewise to set the young boys to
knitting.

Two years later it was agreed that

a woman shall be had from Gloucester further to instruct the
Children in the Pin trade for about two months . . . and her Pay
shall be two shillings or two and sixpence a week. She is to keep
the children to their hours work and to work herself with them.

But this did not entirely solve the problem of the children
living in the workhouse, and two months later came a resolu-
tion that

all the Boys and Girls in the workhouse that are fit to goe
apprentice be put out as soon as places can be procured them.

Much later, in 1819, an agreement was made which must
have provided a welcome breath of fresh air for some inmates,
even if they were still made to work hard. It was resolved to

employ the children or persons out of the workhouse to weed the
churchyard walks.

Looking at the country as a whole, there were wide variations
both in the types of relief granted and in the attitudes of the

officers who administered the poor law. In Upton there was the mixture of kindly and fairly hard-hearted individuals that may be found in any community, as is illustrated by the events of the winter of 1777-8. In December it was resolved that the weekly allowances should be discontinued, anybody who wanted relief being obliged to go into the workhouse. Since this system was, 50 years later, advocated by government policy, it might be claimed that Upton men were quite progressive in their views. However, the new system had numerous disadvantages, not least that it failed to take account of seasonal unemployment which was a particular feature of places like Upton: work in the fields or on the river was plentiful in the summer months, but if a family had been forced to enter the workhouse because of winter unemployment it was in danger of remaining there because the discipline made it difficult to find out, for example, which local farmers were looking for labourers. In addition, the workhouse tended to have a withering effect on the personality so that the incentive to become independent again was frequently subdued. In fact, however, on 5 January 1778—the very day on which the paupers were due to enter the Upton workhouse—the proposal was rescinded, humanity having prevailed:

> The Resolves . . . have been duly considered and it is thought highly improper to put them in execution at this time of year.

Upton does indeed appear to have been a parish in which the administration of the poor law was fairly kindly, with the occasional purge when things started to get out of hand. In 1765 there is an entry which, though patronising, shows some enlightenment,

> To money gave the Poor People in the House at Several Times for encouragement.

Occasionally, too, one finds compassion hidden in the briefly-worded records:

> Feb. 1766   that Mary Kent be reliev'd discretionaly during the frost.

Or there was an attempt to keep a perhaps proud woman from the shame of the workhouse: she was given money in 1765

> for her House rent to keep her from the House.

There was also a degree of laxity about the admission of strangers to the parish. This is revealed by periodic enquiries about newcomers as mentioned on page 59, and in 1782 there was a particularly interesting entry showing the subtle wiles—not in this case of the poor themselves—with which the officials had to cope. It appears that the housing of paupers from other parishes was costing Upton quite a lot of money in uncollectable rates:

> no levies are paid for many of the houses rented by Paupers thro' the Contrivance of the Landlords of such Houses who refuse to pay the levies themselves concluding that the Parish will sooner loose such levies than collect them of such Paupers and thereby make them Parishioners (some of them not having any legal Settlement here). Now it is ordered that the Officer do cause such Paupers to be examined touching the Places of their respective Settlements and that such Paupers as are not settled here be removed.

In November 1800 there was a big effort to sort out the deserving poor from the scroungers. Sixty-two of the more substantial property owners were to form a committee, and as many as possible would attend the fortnightly meetings to be held 'so long as the present high price of provisions shall continue'. The poor were advised to 'attend individually to state their necessities'. Although, in fact, the committee never seemed to reach anything like its unwieldy total, it is nevertheless not difficult to imagine the feelings of the inarticulate poor who faced cross-examination by the comfortable and confident men who exercised the power to grant an allowance or not. On the first day there were 41 applicants: 32 were successful in obtaining help; five were not; and three were given no immediate decision, the cases being postponed for further enquiry. The remaining case was that of a 13-year-old orphan boy who

> was put apprentice at Worcester, ran away, was put in gaol and then taken to the Town Hall and from thence ran away . . . behaved very ill . . . stole a handkerchief.

The committee solved this one by sending the boy back to his master—without apparently trying to find out why he had run away in the first place.

Despite the fact that the committee was made up of unpaid and untrained men it seems on the whole to have applied sound commonsense. A woman struggling to be independent received help—no doubt because the committee saw that in the long run it would save the parish money: so the wife of a soldier who had run off was granted three shillings (15p) a week for her baby

> to place out child to Betty Harbage of Welland, that she may go to service.

An unmarried mother with a two-year-old child did gardening work in the summer, but in the winter 'can only take care of her child'. Her weekly allowance was raised by 6d. to two shillings a week. The wife of a waterman asked for £1 1s. 0d. to pay the half year's rent: the husband earned eight shillings (40p) a week, and they were already receiving two shillings poor relief, but they had four children under eight. She was allowed her rent. But the wife of another waterman earning 11 shillings (55p) a week, with three children, did not get the £2 10s. 0d. she wanted for rent and clothes: she could earn five shillings a week herself as a governess, and they also took in lodgers. The committee seemed quick to sniff out the people who were poor managers: the wife of a bricklayer with a 10-year-old son was given no help because her husband was seasonally out of work in the winter. In summer he earned 'considerably more than will support his family' and about 10 shillings (50p) in winter. The wife was also employed as a laundress. The committee still followed the traditional practice of granting clothing: an elderly widow was granted an outfit— gown, petticoat, shift, apron, handkerchiefs—for her 17-year-old daughter out at service.

In 1834 a far-reaching reform of the poor law took place. The Poor Law Amendment Act grouped parishes into Unions, and Upton became the centre of a Union containing many of the surrounding parishes. A Union Workhouse in Upton replaced the old parochial workhouses and was built and maintained out of rates levied throughout the area. Originally erected in 1836, it was enlarged in 1870 to provide an infirmary. One hundred and fifty inmates could thus be accommodated. By now the steady erosion of government by the parish was starting, and larger, more powerful bodies were to take over, thus introducing a system that provided greater uniformity throughout the country, but less flexibility—and, sometimes, rather less commonsense.

For just over a hundred years the Union Workhouse served Upton and the neighbourhood, the details of its administration changing with successive changes in government policy and public attitudes. After the Second World War, modernised and renamed Laburnum House, its role was altered and it became a home for the elderly. Thirty years later, in 1978, a purpose-built home was constructed—amid controversy as to its architectural merits—across the River Severn at Ryall. At the time of writing, the future of the old workhouse is undecided, and, although it may perhaps be demolished, there are those who would seek to preserve this interesting example of architecture symbolising Victorian ideas.

Chapter VIII

THE SICK

SOME CONSIDERATION of early medical treatment follows on quite naturally from the discussion of ways of dealing with poverty because the old poor books provide evidence of the medical treatment given to the poor. Medical men fell into three classes: physicians, surgeons, and apothecaries, though, as time went on, their functions tended to overlap. A physician often worked from theories and philosophies rather than first-hand evidence—some diagnosed without seeing their patients—and too often the ability to impress rich clients with his good breeding made more impact than an ability to effect a cure. Surgery was grievously hampered not merely by the general condemnation of dissection as an aid in training, but also by the fact that no satisfactory anaesthetic was available until the 1840s, and there are obvious limits to what even the most skilled surgeon can do to a conscious patient. In effect, a surgeon was a swift and skilful butcher, speed and strength being of the greatest significance, and the essentially manual aspects of a surgeon's work made him somewhat lower in social status than the physician. The apothecary was inferior to both. In addition to offering advice he dispensed pills, powders and peculiar brews, which put him in a class of a tradesman rather than a professional man in a society which had a rigid class structure. However, physicians, surgeons and apothecaries all enjoyed a respected status, though actually they were not usually able to do very much for their patients, and probably an experienced 19th-century doctor could do rather less than a raw medical student today. Until the middle of the 19th century medical training was very limited, and, indeed, much of it was irrelevant or even inaccurate.

There are no records of the treatment of the well-to-do in Upton: they will have paid their bills and quietly recovered or expired. But when medical men were called in to treat the poor they were paid out of the poor rates, so the accounts were carefully kept and give us some idea of what they did.

In 1727 Dr. Herbert was called in to perform amputations on a labourer and a boy, though why such surgery was necessary is not known. Possibly a river or farming accident occurred, but one wonders why the patients had to be brought into town, as is recorded:

	£	s.	d.
Paid to Doctor Harbert for cutting off Lippitt's arm and wh he applyed to him before his arm was cutt off and for what he applyed to Margrtt. Palmer in her illness	7	10	0
Paid Doctor Harbert for cutting off the Boys Leg ..	5	0	0
To ten weeks pay for the Boy and Man and one weeks pay for the Boy	3	3	6
For Dyat	1	19	10
Linnen cloth, Burying the Leg and Arm Charcoale, bringing the Old man and Boy to Town		5	6
Paid Joseph Dalby for a Shin of Beef for Lippitt and his boy			6

Fortunately medical treatment was but rarely so disturbing, and in those days death provided a release from the more ambitious attempts of surgeons. For the most part it was a matter of applying various ointments, drinking special herbal brews or submitting to blood-letting. Treatment for psychological disorders was unheard of—the patient was simply restrained from inflicting violence on himself or others. People's expectations of what a doctor could do were not high and, since they were not very effective at providing cures even for physical illness, they did not experience anything like the workload of doctors today. Most midwifery cases were dealt with by female midwives, the doctor being called in only if things became difficult. Childbirth was always dangerous for both mother and child, but in 1719 poor Dorothy Jones had a particularly distressing time: she was in labour for nine terrible days and no-one was able to relieve her pain though she was cared for lovingly with sugar, oatmeal, ale and the considerable luxury of white bread. The ale may have been significant for in the

absence of anaesthetics it was a kindness to induce drunkenness
in a suffering patient. It is hardly surprising that poor Dorothy
Jones died, though her baby lived—for how long is not known.

At the beginning of the 18th century Mr. Beale was the
bone-setter for Upton, and it was to him that Widow Hartlebury
and Bess Griffin's little girl were carried when they broke limbs.
The Aycrigg family figured large in the care of the sick for
about seventy years in the 18th century. Father and son were
medical men, and a Mrs. Aycrigg was paid from time to time
in the 1760s and 1770s for midwifery. From 1714 to the
1780s a 'Mr. Aycrigg' was paid for medical treament, though
it is not clear when Benjamin took over from Charles. The
first references are vague—supplying salve for a lame boy whose
leg had been giving trouble for months, 'tending Jefferyes'
and 'cure of Gibbs leg' were all the work of Mr. Aycrigg. But
later on agreements were made between him and the parish so
we find that in 1761 he was to be paid £6 a year for attending
the poor. The next year, in return for £7, he promised

> to Look after the sick and Lame belonging to ye Parish of Upton
> upon Severn to find them medicenes proper for their Cases and
> Attend them in all Cases of Surgeonry for the Concideration of
> Seven Pounds per Annum.

This agreement, which hardly seems generous to the doctor,
shows the blurring of the old distinctions between the three
classes of medical men for Mr. Aycrigg was acting as physician,
apothecary and surgeon. In 1763 his fee was increased to
£10 and he was called upon, for example, to 'salivate' a
woman and 'cure her of ye foule decease'. Despite such
agreements he made specific charges on occasions like the
'Cure of ffrans. Pumphrey's wife and children when scalded'
in 1764 and in 1766 when he was given three shillings to cure
a man of 'the itch'.

In the early 1760s occurred a most unusual and tragic case
illustrating the fate likely to befall anyone with mental or
psychological problems. The parish spent a lot of money on
a poor woman:

	£	s.	d.
payde for a Lunatick order		2	0
pd for a chain for Marey Edging		1	6
gave Richard Armstrong to Bare his charges to London with Mary Edgen to Bedlam	2	2	0

Various entries concerning Mary Edging lead one to suppose
that she was cared for locally for some months until her
condition became so bad that she was chained and clamped
to confine her. Eventually it was decided to send her to London,
where she was to be kept in the infamous Bethlehem Hospital
which is usually referred to as Bedlam. Conditions there were so
terrible that Bedlam soon entered the language as a term to
describe any scene of chaos and uproar. Until 1770 it was one
of the sights of London, where visitors could pay to watch
the strange behaviour of the inmates and tease them in much
the same way as some people now find so amusing when they
pester the animals in a zoo. Before her departure for London
Mary Edging was provided with a complete set of clothing—
cloak, cap, shoes, gown and so on—and one or two quilted
coats, which were probably strait jackets to restrict the poor
woman's movements. She was certainly tied down in some
way because, as well as her chain, '2 new lasis' were bought
for her. Before leaving Upton she was stripped and washed:
two women accompanied her on the boat to Worcester and
it seems that Richard Armstrong was paid to go with her in
the wagon which was hired for the long uncomfortable journey
to London in the winter of early 1761. The reason is not clear,
but nine months later, in November, she was carried back to
Upton and for two more years small sums were spent on clothes
for her, taking her 'two her Quartores' and so on.

From time to time epidemics occurred. Sometimes they
were referred to vaguely in records as 'the favor' or 'a
pestilence'. Proof of their severity is found in the burial
registers which, though rarely giving the name of the disease,
sometimes show an alarming rise in the number of deaths, as
in 1727 to 1729. But sometimes poor books and registers
specify that smallpox was the cause of death, as in the bad
outbreak of 1693–4. It occurred nationally at that time, and
its victims included Queen Mary herself, wife of William III.
Another outbreak in 1770 hit Upton badly, though there had
been numerous cases during the intervening years. A hint of
better hopes for the future occurs when we read that in 1774
Surgeon Jefferis was paid £2 2s. 0d. for curing a married couple
of smallpox, but the real advance came in 1779. By now
Benjamin Aycrigg's usual annual contract included 'Physick,

Midwifery and Attendance of the Poor' and there was an additional clause: he was to get four shillings

> for the Inoculation of each Pauper that shall be nominated and appointed by the majority of the Paymasters and the Churchwardens and Overseers and the said Mr Aycrigg do agree to provide sufficient Medicines and to take proper care during the Time of the Inoculation.

Another inoculation agreement was recorded in 1784. Inoculation against smallpox, though at first somewhat risky and less effective than the later vaccines which were used, was, nevertheless, a significant development: in fact, it was probably the only 18th-century development in medicine to have any marked effect on the national death rate.

However, there was still a very long way to go and the 19th century saw, for example, outbreaks of cholera, which baffled doctors for years until the patient research of medical pioneers proved to the sceptics that pure drinking water, proper drainage and reasonable standards of cleanliness—both public and private —were vital if such epidemics were to be avoided. Cholera arrived in England in 1832 and boatmen coming up the Severn from Bristol, Gloucester and Tewkesbury told alarming tales of its ravages in those towns. In July the death of an ostler at one of Upton's inns aroused little concern, but about a week later, on 24 July, young Mrs. Jane Allen died after great suffering in her cottage in Lapstone Alley. This narrow alley, running from Dunn's Lane to the banks of the Severn, was dirty and unpaved; most of the cottages were occupied by fishermen who left all kinds of smelly and unhealthy rubbish outside their doors. It was remarked that the disease, which caused the death of about fifty Upton people in one month, had particularly devastating effects in the area around Dunn's Lane and New Street, where there were many narrow alleys and the houses were close-packed and frequently overcrowded. Even in the present century the areas have been badly affected by the Severn flooding, and in earlier ages, prior to strict public health laws, drainage was totally inadequate. We have already seen, from manorial presentments, the lack of real public concern about hygiene—heaps of manure being left in the streets for weeks at a time—and there was apparently an open ditch carrying water and sewage down New Street. There is no evidence to suggest that things had dramatically improved by the early 19th century, so it is small wonder that Upton was visited by cholera. Burial in the graveyards around the old church was forbidden soon after the severity of the outbreak in 1832 became apparent, and this may have done something to control it. From mid-August cholera victims were buried, with scant respect, in Parson's Field, about half a mile beyond New Street, and some distance away from populated parts. The site, now overgrown and desolate, may still be seen, surrounded by a low brick wall with a brief inscription. It is by the site of the old railway track a few yards along the rough path that, according to local tradition, has been called Cut Throat Lane since some obscure day in the 18th century when someone committed suicide there.

Mrs. Lawson, writing when people still had vivid recollections of the 1832 cholera epidemic, has provided a moving account of that time. The last few years of world-wide news coverage of great disasters may have blunted our response to terrible suffering. But Mrs. Lawson was no hardened reporter, and she wrote in a simple and sensitive style of the suffering in this small town of about 2,000 people. They not only suffered pain and bereavement, but were bewildered by a disease which was strange to them, not comprehending its causes and frightened of its effects.

> Jane Allen was a bright, pleasant, little woman, and had been a nurse in Worcester Infirmary, where, however, her experience of sickness had not made her courageous. She was especially nervous and timid about this new disease . . . It is believed that she had been ailing for some days, but no-one about her knew of what deadly significance were those premonitory symptoms, until one July evening, when she was seized with the cramps of cholera. Those who were her neighbours remember how they crowded into her room and fled from it again in horror at her distorted face and limbs, and the pain which nothing could remove or even lessen. They heard her cries almost ceaselessly through the night, and at times they were so shrill and piercing, that the further off neighbours in Dunn's-lane could not rest but came to their doors, full of pity for the poor young creature, and of terror at that which might be coming on themselves. Towards daybreak those agonising cries ceased, and Jane Allen lay all blue and shrunken, but free from pain, till death came some time in the morning of July 24th.
>
> That afternoon, a strong vigorous hay-trusser, William Halford, landed from Gloucester. He looked much as usual but complained of

feeling not quite well; at midnight he became fearfully ill, and although doctors were with him directly, and they and his family knew what the symptoms meant, and tried every means of relief, they could not save his life, nor mitigate the tortures which, in this case, seem to have been unusually severe . . . he died in twelve hours after the cramps had seized him, and was buried that afternoon. Before the grave closed on him there was another case . . .

By the end of the first week in August there had been eighteen burials, and the whole place seemed covered with the shadow of death. There was the frequent carrying of coffins and passage of funerals through the streets, and the almost constant tolling of the bell announcing the passing away of another soul, or the conveyance of another corpse to the church. People watched from afar that spot to the north of the chancel where lime was shovelled on to the coffins, and the faces of the bearers and the white robes of the clergyman looked 'unked'* in the flickering glare of the pitch burned by the grave, when, as happened two or three times, the burial took place after the long summer day had faded into darkness. It was soon decided to forbid further interments in the churchyards, and a piece of the field called Parson's Field, about half a mile from the town, was at once set aside and enclosed . . . One of the first persons buried in the country was a woman by the name of Church, and the man who conveyed the body remarked, as he turned homewards, that 'folk need not fret now about there being never a Church in Parson's Field, for he had put one in himself'. He was attacked that evening, and was almost the next corpse interred; his wife following him in a few hours. One or two similar cases are mentioned in which men or women, probably to disguise their fears, indulged in some such ghastly jestings. It jarred too keenly on their neighbours' overstrung nerves to be easily forgotten or forgiven. Even now the poor foolish jokes are related, with the swift punishment that followed them. No such scoffer, it is said, escaped either death or very dangerous illness, for 'the Lord would not let those alone who made fun of the cholera'.

As the cases of cholera increased, and the fear and peril grew from day to day, the means to counteract them grew also. Clergy and laity met daily to plan fresh precautions, and to grant relief in the most liberal and abundant measure. In a few days a temporary hospital was fitted up in some empty buildings at the back of New-street, and thither, whenever removal was possible the sick were taken on the first symptoms of illness. Abundant supplies of bedding, food and restoratives were sent, and one or other of the medical men was constantly in attendance. But the poor creatures who were brought in would have been very badly off but for the untiring devotion of some non-professional nurses. We have met with no account of those fearful three weeks without hearing one

*lonely, dismal, dreary.

name mentioned with unfailing gratitude and affection—the name of a young solicitor, the late Mr. T. W. Walker, who came at all hours of the day or night, not only to the hospital, but into the miserable cottage rooms, fetid with the sickening breath of the pestilence. He stayed by wretched patients, whose friends, worn out or terrified, could not do the requisite nursing, and he shrank from no task, however hazardous or loathsome, which could lessen pain or give a chance of life . . .

They needed no common courage who could brave the disease then, when its strangeness doubled its terror . . . it was all new; there was the livid blueness of the skin, the visible shrinking and wasting of the body, and, above all, the cramp, which hideously distorted the face and limbs, and caused the most exquisite agony. In some cases there was added to all these symptoms raging delirium, which lasted till the moment of death . . . doctors were quite undecided as to the nature of the disease and its proper treatment. In almost every case large quantities of brandy were given . . .

After the hospital was fitted up people were, in most cases, saved from having the actual death in their houses; but there was, instead, the horror of seeing those who were taken ill borne through the streets. One poor girl is mentioned who was carried by in a cart, so contorted by cramp that one knee was drawn up to the ear, and the body so unnaturally twisted that 'she was in no form like a human being'. In the night the sick could be taken away unseen; but all say that the nights were harder to bear and worse than the day. That August set in with intense heat and close sultriness; frequent bluish mists hung over the meadows at twilight, the nights were dark and chilly, and there was seldom any freshness in the air except at early morning . . .

The tolling of the bell was stopped in a few days by the rector's orders. It was found not only that the healthy were depressed by it, but that the sick, who heard its mournful clang, and thus learnt that cholera had taken another victim, at once lost hope, and with hope lost strength to endure the suffering and the danger. About the same time measures were taken to fit up a sort of hospital in a barn on Tunnel Hill, and to erect tents and sheds on Hook Common for those remaining in houses where death had been. From the day that these were used the plague was stayed. Those who came terrified and ailing, and might soon have sickened in their unwholesome cottages, grew strong with the liberal diet allowed them, and fresh and bright with the pure breezes of the beautiful common . . .

We can form no idea as to the number of cases of cholera; at first very few recovered, while during the last ten days many rallied after extreme suffering, and there were numerous slight cases. Throughout, the disease in Upton was of a malignant character, more horrible in its symptoms and more rapid in its destruction than in any other Worcestershire town. The mortality was not so large in proportion to the population as in some of the closely-inhabited manufacturing parishes; but here each case was known throughout the town, and each death was more or less a grief to numbers of old friends, or neighbours, or relations . . .

It is mentioned, as a sign of the gloom and alarm which hung over the town, that for many days no men stood on the bridge. To anyone who knows Upton, and how our 'bargees' congregate on the bridge from early morning till darkness interrupts their conferences, this avoiding of their usual place of resort shows, more than any-thing else, what a shock to their ordinary habits, what a break in their rough lives, was caused by that time of pestilence. And it is always spoken of now with solemnity and a certain awe, as of some special judgement, and no ordinary illness.

When looking to the past we are sometimes tempted to endue it with a romanticism which is very far from reality. This long quotation from Mrs. Lawson's *The Nation in the Parish* is a useful corrective to the romantically inclined, as significant as the extracts from the earlier manorial presentments. She paints a vivid portrait of the ignorance that bred superstition and fear; of the fact that death was as grievous to the inhabitants of those close-packed and overcrowded cottages as it is to our more sanitised society; and, above all, of the limited extent of medical knowledge which meant that pain and suffering had somehow to be endured without the help of modern drugs and antibiotics.

After the trauma of the cholera in Upton there were several changes. Mrs. Lawson noted the increased sense of community between rich and poor, as well as more material effects such as the provision of more satisfactory drainage and a general cleaning up of the poorer houses. Even so, by the mid–1860s there were still pockets of the town which were unhealthy and in need of proper cleansing and sanitation, for they fell far short even of 19th-century standards. But Parliament was at last paying some attention to the pleas of social reformers who for years had been crying in the wilderness. The provision of proper sanitation and reasonably clean and adequately ventilated housing for the working classes was at last seen as a desirable goal for politicians to aim at, and numerous reforms were instituted. Public health measures resulted in a Rural Sanitary Authority being set up in Upton, headed by a Medical Officer of Health and an Inspector of Nuisances. This became responsible for public health in the area administered by the Rural District Council, which was set up in 1894 and controlled the surrounding villages for the next 80 years, until the controversial 1974 reorganisation of local government. The requirements of successive Public Health Acts produced in the Upton area the same results as elsewhere in the country. Infectious diseases were difficult to control, so epidemics, for example, of measles meant that schools were closed, sometimes for quite lengthy periods, in an attempt to contain the outbreak. More serious diseases like diphtheria and smallpox presented even worse problems, and special hospitals were set up at West Bank, on the Upton-Welland road, and at Welland. Vaccination and immunisation became universal as the 20th century advanced, so that a whole new concept of preventive medicine was added to the more traditional notion of doctors called in to assist the sick. The progress of preventive medicine rendered the isolation hospitals redundant so these were converted into private homes, one of which has for 30 years been occupied by local doctors.

There is some kind of continuity in the more recent years of the history of medicine in Upton. The earliest Medical Officers of Health lived at Willow Bank which was used as a doctors' surgery in Upton until the modern purpose-built block was opened in 1968. Dr. T. Astley Cooper, for many years one of Upton's doctors, and for 17 years chairman of the parish council, still lives at Willow Bank, though the surgery itself is now used as a dental surgery.

Chapter IX

SCHOOLS IN UPTON

WHILST ITS NEIGHBOUR, Hanley Castle, has had a school from medieval times, Upton has no school of such ancient foundation, for in 1662 the churchwardens reported 'yt for scoole houses, Almshouses or hospitalls we have none'. Although in 1667 a Thomas Pitt, 'scholemaster' was buried, this is hardly evidence enough for the existence of a school in the parish.

Early in the 18th century a charity school was founded as a result of bequests made by a very conscientious rector, Richard Smith, and his wife, in 1716 and 1718 respectively. The money was augmented in 1824 by the bequest of Sarah Husband. Surprisingly, the school was for girls and aimed at teaching them knitting, needlework and reading 'in order to qualify them for getting their Bread honestly in the more humble Avocations and Callings'. Clearly there is little prospect here for the industrious to rise above her station in life. A document of 1801 explains that the more advanced skill of writing might be imparted to a girl in her final year at school but 'on no account till she has acquired sufficient skill in Knitting, Working and Reading'.

By this time a more ambitious scheme had been initiated as the result of a £100 gift from a Mr. George Kings of Islington, a man who had already contributed to the rebuilding of the church in the 1750s. This gift, together with various other donations, meant that boys as well as girls could benefit and we can immediately visualise the young beneficiaries on reading one of the resolutions passed at a meeting in 1788:

> The Girls be cloathed in a grogram Gown and Coat and Straw
> Hat Shoes Stockings Shift and Tippett

78

GIRLS CHARITY SCHOOL,

UPTON-UPON-SEVERN, 1801.

THIS SCHOOL was eſtabliſhed by the Wills of Mr. RICHARD SMITH, and Mrs. ANN SMITH, (dated 1716, and 1718,) for the proper Education of at leaſt TWENTY POOR GIRLS of this Pariſh ; and proviſion is made for a Competent Allowance to a Miſtreſs of the School, who is to teach the ſcholars *to Read, to Write, and to Work,* in order to qualify them for getting their Bread honeſtly in the more humble Avocations and Callings.

FIVE TRUSTEES are appointed to Overſee and Manage the Concerns of the Charity : The preſent Truſtees are

Thomas Bland, Eſq. the Rev. Mr. Baines, the Rev. Dr. Evans, the Rev. Mr. Salmon, and the Rev. Dr. Lucas.

But the Truſtees (on account of their diſtant Reſidence) not being able to give that conſtant attention to the Inſtitution which it requires, have appointed THREE STEWARDS, Reſident in the Town, who will inſpect the conduct of the School, and manage the concerns of the Charity ; rendering once every year, an accompt thereof to the Truſtees, who will readily attend in perſon as often as occaſions may require. The Preſent STEWARDS are

James Skey, Eſq. Mr. Thomas Huſband, and the Rev. Mr. Hutchinſon.

Mr. THOMAS HUSBAND receives the Rents and keeps the Accompts of the Charity.

On the 17th *of February,* 1801, *Mrs. Ann-Fildes was appointed Miſtreſs of the School.*

The following Regulations have been agreed upon by the Truſtees ; and the Stewards are fully authoriſed to ſee that they be properly and regularly obſerved by all who are concerned.

R U L E S.

I.

THAT the Miſtreſs do regularly attend the School at the following times,—from 9 till 12 in the Morning ; and from 2 till 4 in the Afternoon.

II.

THAT the Miſtreſs do teach the Children to Knit, to work with the Needle, to Read, and to Write ; and alſo to repeat the Church Catechiſm.—No Child is to be taught *Writing*, till within one year of her quitting School ; and on no account till ſhe has acquired ſufficient ſkill in *Knitting, Working, and Reading*.

III.

THAT the Miſtreſs do conduct the Children to Church regularly every Sunday, and ſee that their behaviour be becoming ; and correct, as much as lies in her power, any thing improper in their general deportment out of School Hours.

IV.

THAT no Child can be admitted under ſix years of age ; nor be allowed to continue in the School longer than four years ; nor ſo long, if deemed ſufficiently inſtructed to make room for others.

V.

THAT the Parents of the Children be careful to ſend them to School and to Church combed and waſhed, and in decent apparel.

VI.

ALL Perſons, wiſhing to have their Children admitted into the School, muſt apply to the Stewards ; and all who wiſh to withdraw them, muſt give a week's notice, that others may be elected in their ſtead.

VII.

The Stewards may diſmiſs any Child for improper behaviour ; and, as much of the uſefulneſs, as well as extent, of the Charity will depend on the Children coming *regularly* to School, they may alſo be diſmiſſed for habitual *Non-Attendance*, unleſs ſome reaſonable cauſe thereof be aſſigned.

VIII.

THAT the Holidays of the School ſhall be as follows :

At Eaſter, *one week*,	Founder's Day, 24th *June*,
Whitſuntide, *one week*,	At Harveſt, *three weeks*,
May-Day,	Chriſtmas, *two weeks*,
King's Birth Day.	

No School in the Afternoon on Saturdays.

W. DYDE, PRINTER, TEWKESBURY.

Girls Charity School Rules

while

> the Boys be cloathed with Coats, Waistcoats Breeches Shoes Shirts
> Hat and Stockings.

The children were not clad in cast-offs or second-hand
clothing, as might well have been the case: various tradesmen
in Upton were paid for 'making cloaths' and for hats and
shoes, and, early in 1790, seventy pairs of shoes were ordered
from Bristol and presumably brought up river by trow. The
clothing was probably of as much significance to the children
as the education they received, for, though like children of
every generation, they no doubt expressed dissatisfaction with
their uniform, it seems to have been practical and warm—
qualities to be appreciated in poor homes with hard-pressed
parents struggling on a tight budget to bring up large families.
During the first year the outfit was worn only on Sundays
but afterwards

> the clothes shall be given them if they are in the school and shall
> have behaved themselves well.

The uniform meant that the children were all decently clad
for their strictly disciplined Sunday occupations; no hint of a
five-day week was to be heard for many years.

> On Sunday the children shall attend public worship, under the
> eye of the master or some of his family, or their parents, unless
> prevented by illness or any other sufficient cause; and after divine
> service shall return to the school-room, and shall be set to learn
> some portion of scripture or other proper book.

Bibles and other necessary books like spelling books were
provided for the children and became their personal property
after two years, though, like the clothing, with the proviso
that they had behaved themselves. The standards required of
the master were also quite demanding, for he had to be
'tender in correcting them' and to 'take all possible care to
prevent impiety and immorality'. His performance was kept
up to scratch by regular inspections by members of the
governing body which was anxious to ensure that

> the utmost care be taken to bring up such children honestly,
> virtuously and religiously.

33. This building in Court Street is believed to have been Upton's Workhouse, purchased by the parish in 1764.

34. The Old Court House, built in the early 19th century, gave Court Street its name.

35. & 36.   Two views of the Union Workhouse,
built in 1836 and extended in 1870. It served
Upton and its surrounding parishes.

37. A very old picture – about 1850 – of the end of Old Street, showing the turnpike gate and toll cottage. Upton Turnpike Trust was founded in 1752.

38. The end of Old Street became known as Station Road during the late 19th century.

39.   Upton railway station, opened in 1864.

40.   The site of the railway station in 1977 – a council yard. It is now (1988) used as trading units and for light industry.

41. Old Street, *c.*1910.

42. Old Street, looking towards the centre of Upton. This old postcard dates from about 1910.

43. High Street, about 1900.

44. High Street, about 1920. Note how the tree at the corner of the old churchyard had been lopped since the previous picture was taken.

45. High Street: a slightly later view. The main road still continues straight down to the old bridge near the *Star*.

46. High Street in the early 1970s: the garage next to the *White Lion* has now disappeared.

47. & 48. The *Talbot* (*c.*1910) has now become the *Talbot Head* and undergone some changes.

49. High Street (river end) about 1910. There is a marked similarity between this picture and a drawing made in 1868.

50. Ham Court, home of the Martin family, in the 19th century.

51. The old brickworks on the far side of the river, about 1860.

52. The old gasworks in New Street, about 1930.

53. & 54.   The Mount, at the top of Tunnel Hill, at the end of the 18th century, and in the 1970s.

55. & 56. The cholera burial ground in the winter of 1978.

57. The end of New Street, about 1870. The curious castellated building was known as Limerick Castle.

58. The end of New Street, about 1886. A brick building had recently been erected between the older buildings on the left.

59. & 60.   Two views of the *Bell* about 1920 and 1975.

61.   New Street, about 1920.

62.   New Street in 1979.

63. Mrs. Emily Lawson, Upton's first historian and wife of the Rev. Robert Lawson, rector of Upton 1864-1895.

64. A modern picture of one of Upton's alleys. There used to be many such alleys, with considerable overcrowding in the houses encouraging the spread of disease.

The money to finance the school came from benefactors like George Kings, and annual subscribers, who paid up to a guinea (£1.05p) a year and were kept informed of the school's progress at quarterly meetings. The governing committee met every month either in the workhouse or in the 'coffee room'. Ladies and other subscribers living more than two miles away were spared the embarrassment of actually having to appear in such meeting places: they were allowed to vote by proxy— though the most controversial decisions seem only to have been who should or should not be admitted to the school.

Any benefactor or subscriber could recommend a child for admission, and preference was given to the most necessitous cases and to children whose families had long been settled in the parish. The school educated those between the ages of seven and twelve, though no child stayed longer than three years, and 'no child shall be admitted who is not free from any infectious distemper'.

By 1801 the holidays had been somewhat modified, but from the very beginning the tradition of a harvest-time holiday was established, to be taken 'at such time as shall be thought the most advantageous'. Boys and girls were taught separately, and according to an agreement of 1797 the boys' schoolroom was 19ft. by 14ft. Here, Mr. Orme, in the boys' school since its inception, taught '20 scholars to write and sum and read' for £20 a year, plus £3 for his trouble in providing and fitting up the room, the precise location of which is not clear.

The minutes of a meeting held in March 1825 show that these charity schools (the boys' and girls' departments each being regarded as a school) formed the nucleus of the National Schools set up in Upton. The National Society was founded in 1811 to combine elementary education with indoctrination into the principles of the Church of England, and was very active throughout the country in the 19th century. The 1825 meeting in Upton set the hours at 9 a.m. to 12 noon, and 2 p.m. to 5 p.m. daily. On Sundays all work was to be of a religious nature since the schools were to 'combine all the advantages of a Sunday School with those of a Day School'. This fact explains why, for many years, the Christmas holidays did not start until noon on Christmas Day, and also why, on occasions, children were punished on Monday for misbehaviour in church the previous day. For some years the schoolmaster was responsible for playing the organ in church as well as his normal teaching duties. In view of the heavy commitment involved for both teachers and pupils it must have been quite a relief for everyone that there were holidays each Thursday and Saturday afternoon, and some shortening of the afternoon sessions during the winter months.

George Griffiths, who in 1852 wrote a survey of schools in Worcestershire, explained that the rector, the Rev. Joseph Martin, had a brick building put up in Buryfield to accommodate the schools. He pointed out that the girls' school had originated in the Smiths' wills and the boys' school had started in the late 18th century, and had been amalgamated with a Sunday School begun in 1812. He also referred to an infants' department. The building in Buryfield was replaced in 1858, as we shall see later.

Charity schools such as Upton acquired in the 18th century provided the only free education available until 1891. Parliament was not interested in education at all until 1833 when it made a small grant to the National Society and its nonconformist counterpart, the British and Foreign Society. Gradually parliamentary grants increased, but not until 1870 did the State take on any responsibility for building and maintaining schools, and even these offered only elementary education. In the absence of government concern, proper inspections and standardised examinations, anybody could set himself (or herself) up as a school teacher, charge fees, and keep going as long as he wanted, or for as long as parents were satisfied that they were getting value for money. Schools seem to have proliferated in Upton during the 19th century, and it is impossible to assess now which were good and which were not. It is a fact that many private schools were very inadequate: in Upton numerous schools, some apparently kept as a sideline by local inhabitants, came and went with the passing years, so it is reasonable to suppose that some, here as everywhere, offered little more than child-minding facilities to harassed parents. Mrs. Lawson wrote that a Mr. Thomas Pitt kept a school, charging sixpence per child per week, which as she herself pointed out, was an extraordinarily high fee. Unfortunately she did not indicate the date, location or even her source of information and it may well be that she was misled; there may have been some confusion with the Thomas Pitt 'scholemaster' already mentioned in 1667.

Nineteenth-century directories refer to numerous apparently short-lived, establishments. John Hart kept a boys' school in New Street, Miss Drinkwater had a school in Old Street, and there was a school 'for gentlemen' kept by Messrs. Wilcke and Worth at Buryfield House. Miss Ainsworth had a humble establishment in Queen Street—regarded as the more high-class end of Dunn's Lane—and Maria Dean and Mary Stallard kept schools in Old Street and Newbridge Green respectively. By the middle of the century the Misses Hudson had a ladies' boarding school in Church Street near the day school of Mary Merryman, and by 1879 Mrs. Briginshaw and her daughter were at Adelaide House, the Misses Huband in Old Street, and Mrs. Pratt, who was also a newsagent, in Old Street. The list might be continued—all kinds of people, including some who could barely read or write, claimed to run schools—but it is fair to point to some of the more tenacious people whose more long-lived schools presumably meant that they were offering reasonable facilities and value. Among these were women like Mrs. Harriet Creese, whose school in New Street survived for over twenty years, and Miss Mary Walton, who kept a day and boarding school for girls at her house in Church Street. Church Street seems to have been quite an educational centre with several schools, and Miss Walton was here for at least thirteen years until she moved to Buryfield Lodge in the 1850s. By 1851 her brother, James Walton, had a boys' boarding school in Church Street, so perhaps Miss Walton thought it undesirable for her young ladies to be in such close proximity to their male counterparts.

It is, however, the National School which stands out as the most useful and continuing contributor to the educational scene in Upton. By 1848 it had become the practice to ask parents to contribute twopence a week for each child, and, although there were always some difficulties in collecting the 'children's pence' it seldom seems to have been a major problem. Occasionally parents made protests about the cost or a teacher's treatment of their child, but this has always been inevitable. In 1847 we see the beginning of what became, nationwide, the standard practice of closing the school gates during school hours, and in Upton this was because certain parents had entered the schoolroom

> to make complaints on various alleged grievances, thereby inter-
> rupting the business of the school, and holding out a pernicious
> example to the children.

By the middle of the century the government had started regular inspections of schools receiving government aid, which gradually increased over the years. In 1857 the inspector wanted the ceilings raised in the rather stuffy schoolroom, and an additional classroom built. But local interest was so fanned that a subscription list was immediately opened, and a completely new set of school buildings, with departments for boys, girls, and infants, was built, and came into use on 21 October 1858. According to the notions of the day, the master of the boys' department was the senior teacher, but the mistresses appointed to take charge of the girls and infants were left to arrange things as they wished in their departments. For long periods a husband and wife team took charge--he as the boys' master and she as mistress of one of the other departments. In 1862, for example, such a couple were to be paid a joint salary of £85, with unfurnished rooms in the schoolhouse, but 'without coals or candles'. School-teaching was not particularly well-paid, and it was no easy profession. In 1866, the three teachers had responsibility for 278 children although, school attendance not yet being compulsory, the average attendance was somewhat lower at 59 boys, 43 girls and 94 infants. Boys and girls were taught together until they reached either the age of seven, or the level of accomplishment which fitted them to enter Standard I. The teachers were assisted by monitors and, if they themselves were suitably qualified, could also have a Pupil Teacher. The monitors were very young; they were local children who had done well at school and had been invited to stay on so that, in return for a few pence a week, they might help to control and teach the children with whom they had so recently shared a desk or bench. Good monitors were sometimes encouraged to become Pupil Teachers. This usually meant going away to another school for practical training under a qualified teacher, drawing a salary during these apprenticeship years of about £7 or £10 a year. It was hard work not only for the monitors and Pupil Teachers who were thus thrown in at the deep end, but also for the qualified teachers who, though naturally glad of all the assistance they could get, had to spend time on a specified number of evenings each week guiding and instructing their young assistants, helping them to become more proficient in the classroom and aiding them to pass the succession of examinations along the path leading to recognition as a fully-qualified teacher.

Government grants to schools were dependent on the individual school's performance in the annual inspections by Her Majesty's Inspectors. This 'payment by results' system meant that the school received a higher grant as its number of satisfactory pupils increased—if too many children did badly the grant was reduced, and there was even the threat of its withdrawal altogether. Upton's log books, therefore, show an understandable concern, shared by all schools, to secure a favourable report. There were desperate attempts to make as many children as possible turn up on inspection day, and to persuade them to attend regularly in the weeks prior to the great day so that they might be drilled and coached for the crucial tests. Since attendance was not legally enforceable until 1880 this could be very difficult and it is as well that in this fairly rural parish the inspection usually occurred in the winter. No rural schools expected good attendance during haymaking or harvest time, for on such occasions parents regarded their children's place as being in the fields, not at a school desk. Blackberries, cowslips, and anything else saleable were hazards to school attendance records in their due season.

The 1870 Education Act was a landmark in the history of education because for the first time the government accepted that in areas where the existing voluntary schools were insufficient, or even non-existent, additional schools should be built and maintained at public expense, locally-elected School Boards being empowered to levy a rate for the purpose. Parishes up and down the land anxiously held meetings like that held in Upton to discuss the implications of the Act. In Upton the National School became a public elementary school. It was resolved to try to supply the necessary additional school

accommodation by voluntary subscription rather than a compulsory rate and to erect a new school at the Hook to serve
the large number of children in and about Brotheridge Green,
Gilvers Lane, and Hook Common. Major Martin immediately
proffered a site; G. R. Clarke, the architect, designed the
building; and Mr. Walker—that courageous helper of cholera
victims nearly forty years before—dealt with the legal aspects.
The school was open within months, things moving remarkably
quickly in those days, and functioned until 1943, when the
teacher became ill. By this time it served only a handful of
children—a symptom of the declining birth-rate and of the
depletion of the rural population—so was closed, the children
and teacher being transferred to other schools and the building
taken over by the authorities to store desks and other school
furniture.

School log books all have a certain similarity in their record
of the day-to-day life of the school, but each has its own con-
tribution to make to an understanding of, not just the school,
but the whole local community. At Upton children barely three
years of age were admitted into the infants' department, and
it is easy to sympathise with all concerned when we read that
the mistress at one point had to request the monitor 'to be
more kind in her manner to the babies'. The noise problem
was clearly considerable with such young children confined in
a room close to where older ones were trying to learn. In 1863
the mistress hit on a novel idea—

> Babies amused by tearing paper—had the desired effect of lessening
> the noise—other classes conducted as usual.

Extremes of temperature could make the room oppressively
hot in summer, while in January 1864 the children were crying
with cold. The vagaries of the stoves with which schoolrooms
of this period were fitted were a universal and often, one fears,
an insoluble problem. Discipline in the crowded rooms was
not easy to enforce, particularly since the teachers did not
always enjoy the support of parents. But they struggled
valiantly to do their best, punishing their charges for using what
they coyly referred to as 'naughty words' or bullying. One girl
was set upon a high form with her pinafore pinned over her
face for disobedience, but punishments are not often specified

so probably amounted to a prompt slap or lash of the cane. Children were as infuriating and ingenious then as ever—in the 1870s George somehow managed to swallow his slate pencil and Thomas pushed a piece of stick up Willie's nose. Though Willie, somewhat given to biting the other boys, could normally be relied upon to look after himself.

The reasoning behind those high-ceilinged schoolrooms of the Victorian age becomes clear when one realises the number of children packed into them. In 1875 the main infant room— 40ft. long by 20ft. wide—was said to provide accommodation for 103 children, while the smaller classroom accommodated 37 in its 300 sq. ft. Infectious diseases spread rapidly even though a child was excluded if he or any member of his family contracted something like measles, scarlet fever, or diphtheria. Skin diseases such as ring-worm necessitated similar precautionary measures. But epidemics of childhood infections inevitably occurred, and in 1894 there was a scarlet fever epidemic despite the efforts of Mrs. Priestnall who wrote after a boy was taken ill in school:

> I have had the classroom well disinfected with carbolic acid, and have hung up a sheet wet with carbolic in the schoolroom. Dr. Cowley visited this morning and examined children who had sore throats.

From time to time the numbers of sick and excluded children made any attempt to carry on school work pointless. Sometimes, therefore, the authorities officially closed the school for a week or two, or sometimes longer. It is difficult to assess whether the true reason for official closure was to try to contain the epidemic or merely an acknowledgement that the thing was already out of hand and that there was little point in trying to teach the few—probably debilitated and anxious— children who had managed to come to school.

The school being a National School, it is understandable that the rector and curate took considerable interest in it, sometimes taking lessons. The womenfolk of their families, including our old friend Mrs. Lawson, were frequent visitors, too, not being averse to trying out their hand at teaching if the staff were unwell or particularly busy. The 'three Rs'—reading, 'riting and 'rithmetic—formed the core of the curriculum, and religious instruction figured large. A lot of effort went into trying to make lessons interesting despite the somewhat regimented methods of teaching which were inevitable with such large numbers of children. There was no room for free expression in those crowded schoolrooms of long ago, but pictures provided the earliest form of visual aid. Talking between the children had to be discouraged, for it would have sounded like a riot with such large classes, but vocal expression in the form of class singing was much indulged in, and a certain amount of energy was used up in drill, which was early, rather formal, physical education. Cookery could not yet be taught, but useful practical crafts like sewing were quite important, and sometimes local ladies made gifts of material for the children to use.

The success of any school is crucially dependent on its staff and, like all schools, Upton had its ups and downs. The perceptive comment of an inspector in 1892 would gladden the heart of any teacher:

> There is an evident sympathy between the teachers and the children which must be at the bottom of all successful education.

This is one of those curiously modern sounding opinions which can take one by surprise when reading the records of the sup- posedly authoritarian Victorians. There were criticisms, even though the school was usually described as one of the best in the diocese, but one wonders just what was expected when the writing is found to be 'a little shaky particularly among a few who have only just turned 3 years'.

In accordance with the terms of the Balfour Act, the County Council took control of the school in 1903 and, in line with the policy of the reforming Liberal government, medical inspections began in 1908. Dr. Mary Williams became a regular visitor and a lot of effort went into raising the standards of cleanliness of all children to the level that most already achieved. Most parents strove hard to keep their children clean, well-fed and tidily dressed, but for years children had occasionally been sent home to wash their hands and faces, or to ask their mothers to provide a clean pinafore. Across the nation a more general awareness of the need for cleanliness became apparent after school medical officers reported an alarming amount of dirt and disease, especially in the more urban regions. Unfortunately, there was still much poverty, and children, even in Upton, had occasionally to stay away while their boots were repaired or their clothes washed.

Patriotism was encouraged, and on Empire Day everyone gathered round the flag to sing the national anthem. Holidays were granted on the occasion of royal weddings, though the children of Upton, in the days before wireless and television sets became universal, can hardly have had much idea of what was going on in such exalted circles.

In 1927 it was announced that the old school departments were to be reorganised into Junior and Senior Mixed schools. By now, due to successive Acts passed in the previous half century, the school, which had extra rooms added over the years, was catering for children between the ages of five and fourteen, though some of the more academic were transferred to the grammar schools of Hanley Castle, Tewkesbury, or Worcester for their secondary education. More social services such as free milk and school meals were also to be introduced as time went on.

Even before the Second World War a purpose-built secondary school for the Upton area had been discussed and an 11-acre site had been purchased. But the war and post-war problems delayed the start of work on the school building until 1956.

The Hill School, designed by Frederick Gibberd, was opened in September 1958 under the headship of Mr. C. J. Prosser. At last Upton had a modern secondary school, just outside the town at the top of Tunnel Hill, 14 years after the Butler Act had required that the 11+ examination should be used in an attempt to provide the secondary education best suited to the needs of individual pupils. The more academic went to grammar schools, while those deemed to require a more practical education went to the Hill School. In 1974 a new system of comprehensive education made the 11+ examination redundant. The Hill School now functions as a Junior High School providing comprehensive education for pupils of all ability groups from the age of 11 until they are fourteen. At 14 they go to Hanley Castle High School, formerly Hanley Castle Grammar School and a school of ancient foundation.

The school in Upton is now therefore a primary school for children up to the age of eleven. Since the 1960s it has been maintained wholly out of the funds allocated by the education committee of the County Council. The Church, which through the old charity and the National Society had financed the building for over a century, gave up responsibility in this respect but retains close contact with the school, being represented on the managing body which every State school in the land is required to have. The rector also visits regularly each week to take prayers. The ease of modern transport and the trend to much smaller families have made it uneconomic to retain rural schools with very small numbers of children, and this has increased the importance of Upton's primary school which no longer serves only the town and parish of Upton. As we have seen, the Hook school was closed during the war, and in 1967 the church school at Ripple was also closed and amalgamated with Upton. Upton school's catchment area is now, therefore, very extensive, and the total number of pupils is about two hundred and fifty.

Chapter X

THE 19th CENTURY AND MODERN DEVELOPMENT

VARIOUS THEMES developed in the foregoing chapters have painted the broad outlines of a picture of a small market town, which, like so many others, adapted with more or less willlingness to the changing times and, particularly in the Victorian era, to the requirements of Acts passed by parliaments with a novel and growing interest in social conditions. In the early 19th century some of the worst features of old

High Street, Upton-upon-Severn, *c.* 1868

Upton, like the open drain in New Street, had disappeared
as had several unsafe buildings like the old cottages in the
corner of the churchyard opposite *The Anchor*. Quite a flurry
of building activity occurred in the 1830s and 1850s—even the
bridge was at long last replaced—and the result caused the 1855
edition of *Billings' Directory* to comment that Upton

> taken as a whole . . . has a very neat and respectable appearance.

The Court House, now (1979) being restored, was built to
serve as a county court which met here once a month until
1867, when the court was transferred to Malvern, which had
grown from a small village to a flourishing spa town as a result
of the efforts of men like Dr. Gully. Upton was also the centre
of a petty sessions district so the magistrates held court here
every other Thursday at 11 a.m. This court was held in the
town hall, now called the Memorial Hall since the 1921 refur-
bishment made in memory of Upton men lost in war. Originally
built in 1832 it was, for its time and for so small a town, a
well-planned and versatile building. The ground floor was
designed as a market house, though it served as such for only
a few years; the well-proportioned room above was used for
court sittings, and in the basement were the gloomy cells used
for the luckless prisoners. Even today, with electric lighting
and incongruously full of children's toys and the other para-
phernalia of the various clubs that use the hall, the cells are
depressing. There is no daylight, the thick brick walls, even
though whitewashed, are forbidding, the cells are poorly
ventilated, and the remains of the iron grilles add to the
generally claustrophobic effect. By the late 19th century the
magistrates' court was transferred to the house in Buryfield
which in the 1860s had been converted for use as the police
station. This, in turn, has been superseded by a modern
purpose-built block. The hall's main function thus became
social: public meetings, concerts, balls and other entertain-
ments took place there. Eventually it incorporated a cinema,
the Rural District Council offices, and a branch of the county
library, the first two now having disappeared, and the library
having now moved across the road to what used to be a cafe.
The Memorial Hall still plays a crucial role in Upton's social
life and is the venue for the local playgroup, dancing school,

amateur dramatics, bazaars and the like, though the more serious business of the parish council is also carried on here, as it has been since 1894 when parish councils were instituted.

Gas lighting was provided in the middle of the 19th century, the gas works being in New Street. The compilers of *Lascelles' Directory* in 1851 were most complimentary about Upton:

> The town is well paved and lighted with gas, and the streets, in which are several very excellent shops, have a very good appearance . . . Races are held annually here, and the course, situated close to the town on the banks of the river, is considered a very good one. There are several excellent hotels and inns, the principal of which are the White Lion and the Star.

In fact, the town was well endowed with both public houses and places of worship—each type of establishment playing, in its own way, a vital part in the life of the community. The Baptist chapel, as we have seen, had long been established, but was enlarged and altered to provide a larger schoolroom in 1863. The Anglican church, too, was practically bursting at the seams, necessitating the erection of another tier of galleries in the 1820s, and, half a century later, its replacement by the new church. Closely linked to the church was the National School, rebuilt on the crest of a wave of public interest in the late 1850s, and near the school was the Catholic Chapel built in 1850. The old Wesleyan chapel was replaced by one put up in New Street in 1891, though this proved to be a short-lived venture. The cemetery in Rectory Road was laid out in 1865-6, and provision made here for two more chapels, the Anglican one being used regularly for Sunday services by the inmates of the nearby Union Workhouse. This helped to prevent overcrowding in the old church and perhaps charity did not go so far as to permit the poor to attend the parish church frequented by those better endowed with the things of this world.

As we saw earlier (p. 66), the Union Workhouse had been built in 1836, and *Billings' Directory* for 1855 was again very complimentary:

> it stands on an eminence, in a most healthy situation, surrounded by a very extensive and beautiful garden.

A mechanics' institute was founded about 1850 and, in keeping with the generally improving character of such establishments

UPTON-ON-SEVERN.

UPTON-ON-SEVERN.

UPTON-ON-SEVERN, a considerable market town and parish, ten miles south-east of Worcester, and seven miles north of Tewkesbury, in the Hundred of Pershore, and diocese of Worcester. This town is very pleasantly situated on the river Severn, which is crossed by a bridge, erected in 1605, but which is now in a very dilapidated state; one arch was destroyed during the Parliamentary wars, when a battery was placed in the church-yard to prevent the forces of Cromwell from crossing the river. The bridge is not considered safe, and it is in contemplation to build a new one. The population in 1841 was 2,696. J. J. Martin, Esq., of Ham Court, is lord of the manor. The town is well paved and lighted with gas, and the streets, in which are several very excellent shops, have a very good appearance. The nearest railway station is that of the Bristol and Birmingham Railway Company, at Defford, about five miles distant from the town. Races are held annually here, and the course, situated close to the town on the banks of the river, is considered a very good one. There are several excellent hotels and inns, the principal of which are the White Lion and the Star; in the former of which it is recorded that the celebrated Tom Jones stopped during his stay in Upton; and the room is now shewn in which it is asserted he slept. The market, which is not very large, is held every Thursday, and the principal support of the town is the traffic on the river Severn, which is very considerable.

THE CHURCH, dedicated to Saint Peter, is a stone erection in the modern style; it has a cupola tower, with a clock and a good peal of six bells. The interior is large and commodious, and has two sets of galleries round three sides of the building. There are no monuments of interest, exeepting a very ancient one, which was saved from the old church, and is now placed in a niche within the communion rails. There is also a good organ. The living is a rectory, in the gift of the Bishop of Worcester. Rev. Henry Joseph Taylor, B.A,, is the rector; Rev. Thomas Wood Hayward, B.A., curate. Mr Robert Harrison, clerk. Time of service, 11 a.m., 3½ p.m.

THE BAPTIST CHAPEL is situated in Old Street, and is a large building, erected about the time the church was formed in 1670; it has galleries on three sides of the building, and will accommodate abot 350 persons. Rev. Alexander Pitt is the minister. Service on Sunday, 10½ a.m., 6 p.m. Thursday, 7 p.m.

THE WESLEYAN METHODIST CHAPEL is a small building at the back of Old Street, supplied by local preachers. Service, 2½ p.m., 6 p.m.

THE ROMAN CATHOLIC CHAPEL, Bury Field, was erected in the present year (1850), and is in the early English style of architecture; it is dedicated to St. Joseph; the cost of the building, about £900, was raised by subscription. At the west end is a small gallery, and over the altar is a painting, representing the Nativity. Rev. J. Walworth, priest. Time of service, 10 a.m., 2½ p.m., 6 p.m.: Thursday 6 p.m.

THE NATIONAL SCHOOLS are situated in Bury Field : they are supported by voluntary subscriptions; they consist of a boys' school, one for girls, and an infant school. Mr. Joseph M. Mansfield, master; Mary Carter, mistress; Jane Millage, infant teacher.

THE STATION HOUSE is situate in Court Street; there are two cells and a house for the inspector. Mr. William Freeman, inspector; Mr. William Probert, police officer.

Upton as described in *Lascelles' Directory* for 1851.

UPTON-ON-SEVERN.

THE TOWN HALL, in Old Street, is a handsome building; it has a market house underneath, and a very good room over it, in which concerts, balls, &c., are held, and where the magistrates hold the Petty Sessions every alternate Thursday, at 11 a.m.

THE COUNTY COURT is held once a month at the Court House, which is a very neat building erected for that purpose, Benjamin Parham, Esq., judge; Thomas W. M. Holland, Esq., assistant clerk; T. W. Ross and J. A. Ross, bailiffs.

THE POST OFFICE is in the High Street; Mrs. Sarah Day, post mistress.

There is a MECHANICS' INSTITUTION formed about twelve months since; the present number of members is about 70. The Library contains nearly 200 volumes, the greater part of which have been very kindly presented by the neighbouring clergy, gentry, and honorary members of the institution.

The members meet for the present in a room at the secretary's house, which is opened for reading, discussion, and exchange of books, every Wednesday and Saturday evenings, from 6 o'clock until 9. Lectures are also delivered every month during the winter season. President, Rev. H. J. Taylor, rector; treasurers, George Clarke, Esq., and Mr. Richard Goodall; secretary, Mr. J. W. Read; Librarian, Mr. Thomas Pratt.

THE UNION WORKHOUSE is a large and commodious brick building, situate near Bury Field, about a quarter of a mile from the town, it was erected in 1836. Richard Temple, Esq., chairman; Mr. William Bathurst, master; Mrs. Caroline Bathurst, matron; Rev. T. W. Haywood, chaplain; Messrs. H. B. Marsh and C. E. Sheward, surgeons; Charles Grave Walker and James Duncocks, relieving officers; George Whitesides, school master; John Skey, Esq., clerk; board days every alternate Thursday.

CLERGY, GENTRY, &c.

Allen Rev. Charles, M.A., The Hill
Couchers the Misses, Bury field
Cowley Mr. Charles, Newbridge gr
Crees Miss Elizabeth, The Bank
Crees Mr. William, sen., New st
Davis Henry, Esq., Uley
Davis Mrs., Bury field
Detheridge Mr. Isaac, The Gardens
George Mrs. Mary, High st
Grise Rev. Thomas, The Mount
Handy Mr. Francis, The Hill
Hayward Rev. Thomas Wood
Hernloch Miss Mary, The Bank
Kent Benjamin G. Esq., Levant lodge, Earls Croome
Kent Cheselden, Esq., Longdon lodge
Kent John Clarke, Esq., Bury field house
Lilley Mr. Thomas, Old st
Martin Joseph John, Esq., Ham court
Matthews Miss Elizabeth, Kent cottage
Pitt Rev. Alexander, baptist minister, The Parsonage, Old st
Simmonds Mrs. Mary, The Eades
Strode Colonel C. Henry, Heath house
Tayler Rev. Henry Joseph, B.D., Rectory
Warren Mrs. Susannah, Bury field
Widdicombe Mr. Richard, Newbridge gn
Williams Mr. Edmund, Elm villa
Woodward Major, The Hyde

POST OFFICE, High Street—*Mrs. Sarah Day* postmistress. Delivery, 8 a.m. and 6 p.m. Letters must be posted before 9½ a.m., aud 5¼ p.m. Money Order business attended to from 9 a.m. to 5¼ p.m.

COACHES.—MALVERN, *Royal Mail*, Star, High st, daily, 5¾ p.m.—TEWKÈSBURY AND CHELTENAM,—*Royal Mail*, Star, High st, daily (Sundays excepted). 10 a.m.—WORCESTER, *Star*, Star, High st, Wed. and Sat., 0 a.m.; *Mail Cart*, Star, daily, 5¾ p.m.

CARRIERS.—PERSHORE, *Done Samuel*, Star, High st, Thursday, 3 p.m.—WORCESTER, *Lyse James*, Old st, Wednesday and Saturday, 8½ a.m.

which sprang up all over the country in the 19th century, the Upton Institute had a library of

> nearly 200 volumes, the greater part of which have been very kindly presented by the neighbouring clergy, gentry, and honorary members of the institution. (*Lascelles' Directory* 1851.)

Sometimes it is difficult for members of a more egalitarian society to come to terms with the fact that, despite the patronising attitudes of the more affluent members of 19th-century communities, their intentions were usually commendable. They lived in comparative comfort, but were, in a sense, the victims of a rigid class structure. The more unfortunate victims were, of course, the poor men, women and children struggling to keep body and soul together. We get some idea of the class-ridden society from the style adopted by 19th-century writers like John Noake, and from directories:

> The lower orders of the inhabitants are much contaminated by contact with large numbers of bargemen who are always lurking about the town, and whose occupation is continued on Sundays. (Noake, *The Rambler in Worcestershire.*)

> Clothing Society, established here for assisting the poor in obtaining necessary clothing in winter, and encouraging provident habits among them. (*Bentley's Directory*, 1841.)

The Upton and Ripple Enclosure Act made changes in both the town and outlying parts in the 1860s. Old common land was enclosed, old customs disappeared, and parcels of land were exchanged and re-allocated in the interests of more efficient farming. It had always been the custom to allow a number of animals into the riverside ham and meadow to graze in late summer, and the rents thus collected went to a variety of parish purposes, such as helping the poor or repairing the church. In 1770, for example, it was, as usual, agreed that

> All the Cattle are to be brought to the gate at the Fisher Row and the money to be paid at the turning in.

The hayward had always supervised the animals and ensured that strays or interlopers were impounded until their owners came to collect them and paid the requisite fines. The tithe map shows that the pound, or pinfold, was on the far bank of the river, near the approach to the old bridge. After the enclosure of common land such things became superfluous. The Enclosure Award also provided allotments for the poorer people who, having had very limited common rights, did not really benefit from their limited compensation for the loss of these rights, unlike the landowners with larger interests, who were compensated with land that they enclosed. Allotments enabled people to grow vegetables to provide cheap and nourishing food. A recreation ground was also provided by the Award as well as the long-needed and properly laid out cemetery in Rectory Road. The graveyards near the old church and the Baptists' burial ground behind their church in Old Street had long been felt to be inadequate and, of course, special arrangements had been necessary in the 1832 cholera epidemic.

In the later 19th century a new cattle market was set up behind the *White Lion* which by the turn of the century boasted such refinements as tennis courts and quoits grounds. *Littlebury's Directory* for 1879 shows that Upton was still important as a market town attracting farmers and dealers from far afield, for the Upton area was 'celebrated for excellent pasturage'. By now river trade was on the decline, while the railway took a lot of traffic. In 1841 *Bentley's Directory* had listed 21 boatowners and coal merchants, but by 1879 there were only two boatowners, though 11 coal merchants and dealers were listed. It is true that some of these were down by the riverside and bridge where coal and other commodities had been arriving for so long, but dealers like Edward Twycross showed the new trend—his premises were at the railway station and in Old Street.

Many men found work on the land as farm labourers and in market gardening, while within the town various trades and shops provided opportunities for work. Some of these were specific to the district: the brickworks on the other side of the river were still in operation though they were later to fall into disuse. In recent years the area has been a rubbish tip and at long last has been given a new lease of life by the building of the marina which points very firmly towards the Severn as a vital aspect of Upton life and history. The cider and vinegar works of the Kent family employed many hands for a very long period from 1778; their business extended to the importing of foreign wines and spirits. The premises, near the approach to the modern bridge, are now occupied by the Regal Garage.

By 1879 the Working Men's club was open every evening except Sunday, providing for more than 80 members not only social contact but also books and newspapers and a 'penny bank' to encourage those provident habits mentioned in the earlier directories. This was the time also of the temperance societies and Upton, with its numerous inns and drinking places, was a natural location for setting up a branch of the Church of England Temperance Society. Other societies included various benefit clubs where, in return for a small subscription, one could draw benefits to help out in times of distress—a common enough arrangement in those days before government controlled unemployment insurance. There was also a mothers' meeting, and, later, a nursing home in Old Street, near to where the telephone kiosk now stands. In this later part of the century the road leading from the end of Old Street past the church to the railway station was known as Station Road—a name now largely forgotten since the demolition not only of that typically Victorian structure, but also of the railway bridge which, according to tales handed down, had been so carefully tested with a slow-moving engine by numerous engineers in the expectant period before the station had been opened in 1864.

The town crier still went about his business from time to time in the late 19th century, but more modern-sounding facilities had also appeared. The present fire station in New Street is very much a product of the 20th century, but some can still remember the old fire brigade with its headquarters in New Street, close to the old pump almost at its junction with High Street. In 1879 this was still a volunteer force and was captained by Mr. Fred Soars, agent at the Lechmere, Isaac, Isaac and Martin bank—the Upton branch for those who wished to conduct their business with the Tewkesbury Old Bank.

For centuries the Martin family were the largest landowners in Upton, and the sale of much of their very considerable estate in 1914 was of great interest and significance. In some cases their former tenants purchased the land and cottages which they had hitherto rented. Ham Court itself, which had been served by local men and women employed as groom, coachman, maid or cook, was put up for sale in 1914, 1925 and 1926. Eventually, in the late 1920s, it was sold to a purchaser who largely demolished it. Various treasures of the house, including fireplaces and staircases, were sold and dispersed all over the world. In the years after world war had shattered so many dreams it was impossible to keep up the style which great landowners had enjoyed in the past.

Times were changing: the right to vote—and, after 1872, in secret—had been granted to all male householders, then to all men and some women, and, at last, in 1928, to all adults. Once the mass of the population had the right to vote in both parliamentary and local elections the pace of social reforms and the provision of public amenities was stepped up. Far-reaching changes were made in 1888 when the county councils were set up, and again in 1894 when the Urban and Rural District Councils, together with parish councils, formed more local tiers in the hierarchy of local government. From 1894 until the next major re-organisation in 1974 Upton was the centre of a rural district council. For many years its offices were in the town hall and adjacent premises in Old Street, but in 1954 they were moved to the former rectory. This old house, at the far end of Rectory Road, had been sold at the end of the 19th century when the church authorities bought from the Martin family the present rectory behind the church. The old rectory was a private house for some time, and its owner decided to rename it 'Old Hall'—an interesting choice since Isaac Taylor's map of 1772 marks in this area the old 'Hall House', which is also mentioned in several parish documents. During the Second World War it was used as a hostel for the land girls who came to work as part of the land army on local farms. Another symptom of war time, apart from many absent sons, husbands and fathers, was the billeting of American forces prior to the D-Day landings, and the setting up of kitchens and a medical unit in the town.

By now Upton had been enjoying for some years modern facilities like electricity and telephones. Some of the old buildings which had become little more than slums were demolished, and, especially in recent years, new housing estates went up. The houses and industrial estate along Rectory Road and the newer estate in Gardens Walk would all greatly

End of New Street, *c.* 1868

surprise those 19th-century inhabitants who knew the whole
area as open land with a house or two dotted over it. They
would find it difficult, too, to recognise the bottom of New
Street, with the modern fire station and the block of flats.
The ancient cottages and the curious building with the equally
curious name of Limerick (or Limbrick) Castle have all gone.
Some attempt has been made to preserve a little of the town's
history: the flats have been given the medieval name of
Collinghurst, and the spot has been marked from which in
1882 were removed the dilapidated Goomstool Cottages, whose
name recalled the memory of one of Upton's less pleasant
aspects—the ducking stool. Nearby the telephone exchange,
opened in 1968, provides modern STD facilities, but gone are
the days of the manual exchange in Old Street when the
operator could advise the caller that there was no point in
trying to put through a call for a few minutes—the person
required had just gone for a cup of coffee.

Every age regrets the passing of old customs—at the same
time feeling a warm complacency about the wonders of new
facilities available to modern man. Upton has had the good
fortune to glide graciously into the modern age. Despite the
fears for the town and its newly-built bridge early in the

Second World War when a little bomb damage was done, neither bombs nor over-zealous planners desecrated the little streets that are packed with history. Perhaps in those streets and their buildings some later researchers will be able to find further material to add to this outline of the development of a fascinating and historic Severnside town.

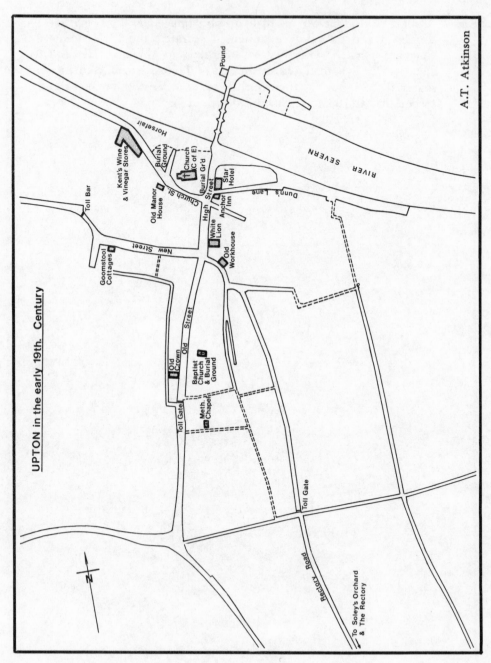

A.T. Atkinson

UPTON in the early 19th. Century

Pound

Horsefair

RIVER SEVERN

Church (C of E)

Burial Ground

Burial Gr'd

Kent's Wine & Vinegar Stores

Old Manor House

Church St.

High Street

Star Hotel

Anchor Inn

Dunns Lane

White Lion

Old Workhouse

Toll Bar

New Street

Goomstool Cottages

Old Street

Old Crown

Baptist Church & Burial Ground

Meth. Chapel

Toll Gate

Toll Gate

Rectory Road

To Soley's Orchard & The Rectory

N

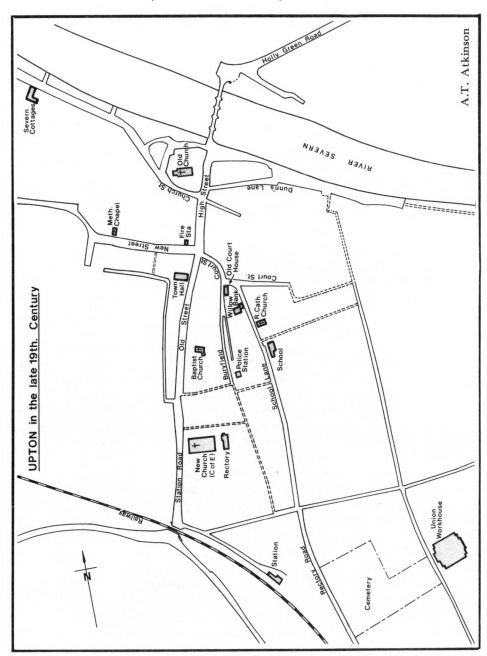

UPTON in the late 19th. Century

A.T. Atkinson

Chapter XI

CHANGE AND REVITALISATION

[*This chapter has been added in 1988 to highlight developments since the first publication of this book in 1979.*]
An important feature of life in Britain in recent years has been a growing awareness of how fragile our inheritance from the past has become. As town centres up and down the land become clones of each other, people living and working in places which have retained individuality and a sense of historical perspective are recognising their good fortune. Like the car once scorned as an old banger and now cherished as a vintage motor, Upton, until recently considered an untidy backwater, has now come into its own as an attractive small town with much to offer both locals and tourists.

In Chapter IV it was suggested that the old church tower by the river might become a heritage centre, and this has indeed happened. Extensive repair work on the tower itself was necessary, and further work provided additional accommodation for a tourist information bureau as well as a display area to illustrate the most important aspects of Upton's history. During the course of this work the inevitable crises and excitements occurred – skeletons briefly attracted police interest but were soon declared to be perfectly respectable 18th-century vault burials – and the centre was officially opened in April 1984. Within three years it was drawing 12,000 visitors a year. Most of the money for this project came from the District Council, based in Malvern, the town which generations of Uptonians have regarded as an upstart rival. This injection of money was particularly welcome – indeed, diplomatic – since Upton has had occasion to feel itself dealt with insensitively by authorities who have not always taken local opinion into consideration in implementing policies which were administratively convenient.

104

The District Council, after local government reorganisation in the early 1970s, firmly centred itself on Malvern, closing the local office in Upton's Old Hall, which was turned into very attractive flats. Upton people found themselves having to travel to Malvern to resolve rate-paying and other problems. Much ill-feeling also resulted from the extraordinary demolition in 1980 of the old Union Workhouse, which disappeared almost overnight. As mentioned at the end of Chapter VII, many people wished the historic building to be preserved but their ideas were as speedily bull-dozed out of existence as was the building itself on that fateful summer weekend. Modern residential accommodation now occupies the site. Another sad, but less substantial, loss was the summerhouse on Tunnel Hill: some inhabitants stoutly declared this to have been an old toll-house – a most unlikely suggestion since no road ever ran within many yards of it – but nevertheless it was an eye-catching landmark dating, as Plate 53 shows, from at least the 18th century. The real and instantly recognisable toll-house at Little Malvern, mentioned in Chapter III, has been given a new lease of life at the fascinating Avoncroft Museum of Buildings, near Bromsgrove in Worcestershire.

A more recent loss (December 1987) was Upton's magistrates' court. Whilst the optimistic might interpret this as a sign that Uptonians must be more law-abiding than residents of other places, others saw it as a further whittling away of Upton's independence. Its modern building, in Buryfields, scarcely arouses the same mixture of bitter-sweet nostalgia as the Victorian workhouse, but a question mark lies over its future use in much the same way as one lay over the old workhouse in 1979: many hope that the authorities have learned a little more tact in the intervening period. Some support has been given to the idea of turning the building into a youth centre but the parish council favours its use as a public library to replace the cramped library facilities in Old Street.

Falling birthrates throughout the country since the introduction of more effective contraception twenty years ago have also had their impact in this area, where provision for secondary education, last overhauled in 1974, is again due for major revision. This will make the Hill School, opened in 1958, redundant. Whilst the loss of the actual building, dismissed by Nikolaus Pevsner as 'nothing special', would hardly be a great

architectural loss, it may in fact be retained – one tentative
suggestion has been its use, in modified form, by the County Fire
Brigade. The real loss will be of the sense of community fostered
by the school. Nearby Hanley Castle High School will become the
sole focus in a wide area for young people from the age of 11 until
they leave school. With centuries of tradition behind it – and over
£1 million worth of building programme already underway – that
school will undoubtedly be equal to the task, but the loss of any
school is always a time for reflection and sadness. For over thirty
years the children of Upton and its surrounding villages were
educated at the Hill School, and such influence is not readily
erased.

Survivors, however, do not sit licking wounds and resenting
losses: they adapt to new needs. Upton is a survivor, and its
historic tower has once more become a symbol – this time of a
response to a modern phenomenon. In late 20th-century Britain
people have more leisure time than ever before and seek a variety
of recreational opportunities. Those Uptonians who opposed the
marina in the early 1970s lacked the foresight that others
fortunately possessed and that was to ensure Upton's survival.
Using the River Severn, that age-old basis of Upton's success, for
a modern purpose, the marina has brought increasing numbers of
tourists to the town. New life was breathed into flagging
businesses and the seeds were sown of a growth industry to meet
the needs of visitors.

Upton's bid for tourists has recently focussed on three main
events: an annual jazz festival, which during a June weekend
attracts about 20,000 people from all over the country; a steam
rally offering a wide variety of nostalgic displays and activities to
some 15,000 people for two days in July; and the increasingly
popular Oak Apple Day at the end of May. Originally a
celebration of the restoration of the monarchy in 1660, Oak Apple
Day was traditionally marked by the ringing of church bells, street
dancing and other customs. Such customs fell into disuse but have
recently been revived in Upton and a few other towns. Like the
local carnival, Oak Apple Day provides a 'fun' day for locals as
well as an added interest for tourists.

'Locals' include not only families long associated with Upton
but also newcomers integrated into the town, many of them living
on the new estates behind the High Street and near the old

workhouse site. But new blood does not mean that Upton is willing to forget its past. On the modern housing estate, carefully preserved tethering rings are a token of the old cattle market on which houses now stand, and the Civic Society has placed blue plaques to focus attention on some of the significant landmarks in the town's long history. Dr. T. Astley Cooper, now dead, is remembered in the cluster of buildings bearing his name near his old home in School Lane. A bust by Worcestershire sculptor, Leslie Punter, has been placed near the Heritage Centre in honour of the local resident Admiral Sir William Tennant, whose family lived at the Eades. He held high office during the Second World War and soon after his retirement became Lord Lieutenant of the county. Many Uptonians and others subscribed to the fund to commemorate one of the parish's most famous sons; his bust stands close to the memorial to the less famous but no less precious sons who fell in war.

Commemorating the past has its rightful place in any community, but safeguarding the future is also of vital importance. If we may judge by its history of constant adaptation to change, underlined by its regeneration in the last ten years, Upton's future would seem to be secure.

BIBLIOGRAPHY

Abbreviations
W.H.S. = Worcestershire Historical Society
W.R.O. = Worcestershire Record Office

Principal Sources
Domesday entry for Ripple and Upton.
Lay Subsidy Rolls for Worcestershire. Translated and published by W.H.S. 1895.
Registers of the Bishops of Worcester. Translated and published by W.H.S.
Household roll of Bishop Swinfield. Translated and published by the Camden Society, 1854.
Itinerary of Leland in the 1530s.
Habington's Survey of Worcestershire in the 17th century, (published by W.H.S., 1895).
Manorial records in W.R.O.: court rolls and presentments.
T. R. Nash, *Collections for a history of Worcestershire* (1799).
Parish papers and books, now in W.R.O., including
    Parish registers since 1546
    Overseers' account and minute books
    Churchwardens' accounts and presentments
    Deeds
    18th-century Charity school rules and records.
Baptist Church minute books.
Roman Catholic Church log book and papers.
Bishop Hurd's Survey of the Diocese of Worcester 1782-1808, ed. by Mary Ransome and published by W.H.S., 1968.
Census returns.
School log books and papers.
Nineteenth century directories.
Tithe Award and map.
Enclosure Award and map.
Isaac Taylor's map of Worcestershire (1772).
Christopher Greenwood's map of Worcestershire (1822).
Upton Turnpike Act and the minute books of the trust.
Quarter Sessions papers in W.R.O. and the Calendar of Q.S.P. ed. J. W. Willis-Bund and published by W.H.S.
Bibliography of Worcestershire ed. J. R. Burton and F. S. Pearson and published by W.H.S.
Ham Court papers in W.R.O.
Ham Court sale catalogues.
G. B. Grundy, *Saxon Charters of Worcestershire* (Birmingham Archaeological Society, 1931).

E. M. Lawson, *Records and Traditions of Upton-upon-Severn* (1869, Houghton and Gunn); *The Nation in the Parish* (1884, Houghton and Gunn).

John Noake, *Rambler in Worcestershire* (1851); *Guide to Worcestershire* (1868); *Worcestershire Sects* (1861); *Worcestershire Relics* (1877); *Worcestershire Nuggets* (1889).

E. P. Shirley, *Hanley and the House of Lechmere* (1883, Pickering).

T. C. Turberville, *Worcestershire in the 19th century* (1852).

Victoria County History (published by Constable) and the notes made by the researchers and deposited in W.R.O.

J. Pumfrey, 'Pumfrey's Upton' (unpublished).

Other sources used for comparative study

J. Allies, *Antiquities and Folklore of Worcestershire* (1852).

J. H. Brazil, *London Weather* (H.M.S.O., 1968).

J. W. Willis-Bund, *The Civil War in Worcestershire* (Midland Educational Company, 1905).

John Chambers, *Biographical Illustrations of Worcestershire* (Prowett, 1820).

R. Disley, *Upton upon Severn, commemorative brochure* (Home Publishing, 1974).

E. Ekwall, *Dictionary of English Placenames* (Oxford, 1966).

R. C. Gaut, *History of Worcestershire Agriculture* (Littlebury, 1939).

V. Green, *History of Worcester* (2 vols., 1796).

G. Griffiths, *Free Schools of Worcestershire* (1852).

N. Hone, *The Manor and Manorial Records* (Methuen, 1906).

A. E. E. Jones, *Anglo-Saxon Worcester* (Ebenezer Baylis, 1958).

F. C. Laird, *Worcestershire* (1818).

A. Mawer and F. M. Stenton, *Placenames of Worcestershire* (C.U.P., 1927).

J. Richardson, *The Local Historian's Encyclopaedia* (Historical Publications, 1975).

J. Ivimey, *History of the English Baptists* (1814).

A. H. Smith, *English Place Name Elements* (C.U.P., 1956).

W. E. Tate, *The Parish Chest* (C.U.P., 1969).

L. Stephen (ed.), *Dictionary of National Biography* (Smith, Elder, 1885).

Additional Reading

W. Salt-Brassington, *Historic Worcestershire* (1894).

G. Miller, *Parishes of the Diocese of Worcester* (1890).

A. MacDonald, *Worcestershire in English History* (Press Alliances Ltd., 1943).

J. S. Leatherbarrow, *Worcestershire* (Batsford, 1974).

R. Corbet-Milward, *The Anglican Churches of Upton upon Severn; Upton in the Severn Valley* (Upton Heritage Festival, 1975).

B. S. Smith, *History of Malvern* (Leicester University Press, 1964).

Peter Smith, *Waterways Heritage* (Luton Museum, 1972).

W. S. Symonds, *Hanley Castle* (1883); *Malvern Chase* (1887).

V. Waite, *Malvern Country* (Phillimore, 1979).

J. West, *Village Records* (Macmillan, 1962).

INDEX

(Numbers in italics denote a plate)

Soley's Orchard, 55, *30*
Southend, 2, 8, 55
Star Inn, 26, 28, 29
Surgeons, 68, 69, 70
Swan Inn, 28, *11, 12*

Talbot, or Talbot Head, 18, 28, 62,
   47, 48
Taxes, 8
Taylor, Isaac, 5, 99
Telephone Exchange, 100
Toll houses, 25
Tower, 33, 34, 35, 36, 40, 46
Town Hall, 92
Trow, 13, 14, 15
Tunnel Hill, 25, 29, 75
Turberville, T. C., 13, 19
Turnpike, 22, *37*

Vaccination, 72, 77

Weighbridge, 25, *23*
Welland, 1, 3, 77
Wesleyans, 45, 93
Wharton, Fr., 43
Wheatsheaf Inn, 28, 62
White Lion Inn, 26-7, 28, 97
William the Conqueror, 3, 7, 9
Willis-Bund, J. W., 19-20
Willoughby, John, 35
Willow Bank, 73
Woodford, William, 32-3
Worcester, Bishop of, 1, 3, 4, 7, 30,
   32, 45
Workhouse, 62-4, 66-7, 93, *33, 35,
   36*
Working Men's Club, 98